The Logos of the Living World

gROUNDWORKS |
ECOLOGICAL ISSUES IN PHILOSOPHY AND THEOLOGY

Forrest Clingerman and Brian Treanor, *Series Editors*

Series Board:

Harvey Jacobs	Catherine Keller	Norman Wirzba
Richard Kearney	Mark Wallace	David Wood

The Logos of the Living World

Merleau-Ponty, Animals, and Language

Louise Westling

Fordham University Press | *New York 2014*

Copyright © 2014 Fordham University Press

All rights reserved. No part of this publication may be reproduced, stored in a retrieval system, or transmitted in any form or by any means—electronic, mechanical, photocopy, recording, or any other—except for brief quotations in printed reviews, without the prior permission of the publisher.

Fordham University Press has no responsibility for the persistence or accuracy of URLs for external or third-party Internet websites referred to in this publication and does not guarantee that any content on such websites is, or will remain, accurate or appropriate.

Fordham University Press also publishes its books in a variety of electronic formats. Some content that appears in print may not be available in electronic books.

Library of Congress Cataloging-in-Publication Data is available from the publisher.

Printed in the United States of America
16 15 14   5 4 3 2 1
First edition

Πᾶσι Τοῖς Ζῴοις

(For all the animals)

Contents

	Acknowledgments	*xi*
	Introduction	1
1	A Philosophy of Life	13
2	Animal Kin	45
3	Language Is Everywhere	101
	Conclusion	135
	Notes	*145*
	Bibliography	*167*
	Index	*181*

Acknowledgments

No one in my generation started out in ecocriticism, because the field did not exist. As I moved from traditional literary scholarship into environmental criticism and interdisciplinary alliances with philosophy and the sciences, I was fortunate to work in a university that is unusually hospitable to such cooperation. Work for this book took me far outside my formal training and depended on colleagues in many different fields, sometimes in completely different professions. Thus I am happy to thank a wide range of interdisciplinary mentors. As my explorations proceeded, colleagues in philosophy have been most helpful and willing to include literary people in their department's activities. Mark Johnson's work on embodiment, language, and art has offered crucial grounding for my thinking. Collaborating with him in an interdisciplinary course opened important connections among cognitive neuroscience, literature, and philosophy. For the past decade Ted Toadvine has been a generous and challenging guide to Merleau-Ponty's work, as well as wider topics concerning environmental philosophy. He and biologist Brendan Bohannan kindly allowed me to sit in on their course on "The Philosophy of Ecology" several years ago, an exciting enterprise involving graduate and undergraduate students in fields ranging from English and philosophy to biology, environmental studies, and political science. I am especially grateful to Annabelle Dufourcq of the Charles University in Prague for sharing her expertise on

Husserl and Merleau-Ponty during her year as a visiting scholar at Oregon and for reading the manuscript of this book with judicious suggestions and moral support.

The Association for the Study of Literature and Environment has provided a lively international community of ecocritics from its beginnings two decades ago, and its biennial conferences have provided opportunities to share many early explorations of Merleau-Ponty's work and his relationship to Heidegger as an environmental thinker. My senior colleague Glen Love was the insipiration behind the creation of ecocriticism as a field and its development in the English Department at Oregon. I am indebted to his support over the years and his urging that environmental criticism engage seriously with the life sciences. Bill Rossi, Gordon Sayre, Suzanne Clark, and Jim Crosswhite have been allies in environmental teaching and research in our department. I also owe much to my colleagues in the University of Oregon Environmental Studies Program and our interdisciplinary collaboration. Alan Dickman, ENVS director, has provided exciting teaching assignments and has been an unfailing supporter of new ideas in environmental scholarship.

Colleagues in ASLE-UK and Ireland and corresponding associations in Australia/New Zealand and Europe have been invaluable interlocutors at conferences in their countries. Special thanks to Greg Garrard, John Parham, Richard Kerridge, Terry Gifford, and Axel Goodbody in the UK; Sylvia Meyer, Heike Shaeffer, and Ann Catherine Nabholz in Germany and Switzerland; and Kate Rigby in Australia. Timo Maran first introduced me to Jakob von Uexküll and biosemiotics, providing some of the earliest links with environmental literary study. Wendy Wheeler has defined bold perspectives on new approaches to cultural history made possible by biosemiotics. I am grateful to her for exciting conversations about this new field and for her reading of the manuscript of this book with complete understanding of what is at stake.

Graduate students in the University of Oregon English Department and Environmental Studies Program have challenged and enriched my understanding of Merleau-Ponty, the animal question, and literary animals in many ways. In particular I want to thank Sarah McFarland, Janet Fiskio, Sean Williams, Kelly Sultzbach, Steve Rust, and Lisa Lombardo.

Mentors and friends in the herding community have shared their understanding of cross-species cooperation among sheep, dogs, and humans that is possible only with respect for other animal ways of being. All these companions in muddy fields and Pacific Northwest weathers have offered encouragement and models of patience and grace in dealing with the difficulties and failures that make up so much of the effort to learn to do this work. Simon Leaning, Chris Soderstrom, Elsie Rhodes, Dave Vicklund, Lora Withnell, Laura Vishoot, Derek Scrimgeour, and Patrick Shannahan have been wonderful teachers. Dave Larson, Karyl Hansen, Pam Carter, Cynthia Mills, and Susan Crocker deserve special thanks for their camaraderie. Esther Jacobson-Tepfer has graciously shared her professional expertise in archaeology and prehistoric art of central Asia as a colleague interested in human/animal relations and her companionship as a fellow sheep herder learning the mysteries that make up the communicative dance between predator and prey animals.

I am grateful to Helen Tartar, Editorial Director at Fordham University Press, for supporting this book and to Assistant Editor Tom Lay and Managing Editor Eric Newman for shepherding it through the production process. As reviewers for the Press, Glen Mazis and Alfred Siewers gave the book wonderfully generous evaluations.

Several pieces of this book appeared in earlier versions.

A much briefer version of Chapter 1 was published as "Merleau-Ponty's Ecophenomenology" in *Ecocritical Theory: New European Approaches* by the University of Virginia Press in 2011 and is presented here with their kind permission. (Goodbody, Axel, and Kate Rigby, eds. *Ecocritical Theory: New European Approaches*, pp. 126–138. © 2011 by the Rector and Visitors of the University of Virginia. Reprinted with permission of University of Virginia Press.)

The editors of *Anglia* have permitted me to reprint a slightly revised discussion of *The Epic of Gilgamesh* and Euripides' *Bakkhai* from "Darwin in Arcadia: Brute Being and the Human Animal Dance from Gilgamesh to Virginia Woolf" in Band 124, 2006.

Some of the arguments about the relationship between Heidegger's and Merleau-Ponty's ideas about animals appeared in "Heidegger and Merleau-Ponty: Ecopoetics and the Problem of Humanism" published in *Culture, Creativity, and Environment: New Environmentalist Criticism*, edited by Fiona Becket and Terry Gifford in 2007, and Rodopi has kindly permitted its reprinting (http://www.rodopi.nl/senj.asp?BookId=NCL+5).

The Johns Hopkins University Press has permitted the use of passages from a 2010 article on "Merleau-Ponty's Human-Animality Intertwining and the Animal Question" published in a special ecocriticism and biology issue of *Configurations* edited by Helena Feder. (Copyright © 2011 by The Johns Hopkins University Press and the Society for Literature and Science. This article was first published in *Configurations* 18.1–2 [2010], 161–180. Reprinted with permission by The Johns Hopkins University Press.)

Finally, I thank Sarah Gordon for sensitive reading, and my husband, George Wickes, for unfailing support as I struggled to discover where this project was going, for listening to endless ramblings about Merleau-Ponty, for accompanying me to inclement herding clinics and trials, and never losing hope that the enterprise might succeed. Alice Springs, Sydney, and Melbourne have been patient and joyous companions and teachers about other ways of being, and Lady Glencora has gradually initiated a truce that gives the lie to Derrida's description of his cat while endorsing Montaigne's.

The Logos of the Living World

Introduction

Playwright Eugene Ionesco described archaic humans as living in "a time, long, long ago, when the world seemed to man to be so charged with meanings that he didn't have *time* to ask himself questions, the manifestation was so spectacular." He claimed that at some point closer to our own era, a break occurred and we lost that sense of plenitude. "We were abandoned to ourselves, to our solitude, to our fear, and the problem was born. What is the world? Who are we?" Similarly, Jacques Derrida asked at the end of his career, "Who am I?" and thus recast Montaigne's famous question of "What do I know?"[1] Derrida's skepticism reaches into the center of humanist confidence in the grand place of *Homo sapiens* at the top of creation. Why did Derrida suddenly devote the last years of his philosophical life to the question of our place among all the other animals? Humanity now covers the earth and seems to dominate its being, but growing awareness of ecological devastation of landscapes and species, even of the vast seas, ice-bound poles, and the climate, lends urgency to the reevaluation of human status that twentieth-century philosophers and environmentalists have demanded. Cary Wolfe sees the humanities as having been left behind in a radical reevaluation of our relation to nonhuman animals that has taken place in popular culture and indeed in many scientific disciplines.[2] The present work offers an interdisciplinary ecocritical argument that phenomenologist Maurice Merleau-Ponty actually began such a reevaluation more than sixty years ago, laying a theoretical foundation that is intertwined with the modern life sciences. Such an approach brings philosophical rigor to ecocritical theory, demonstrates how literary works can illuminate theoretical debates in richer ways than explicit theoretical argument, and brings scientific studies of animals into dialogue with the humanities. Attention to Merleau-Ponty's work reveals why the animal question is more than what Wolfe calls "the central problematic for contemporary culture and theory" (ix) and indeed lies at the heart of a genuinely ecological perspective on the place of human language and culture in the phenomenal world. Environmental thought commonly recognizes that the notion of our species's separation from nature is a mistake that has led to the present crisis, yet environmental humanists and ecocritics have not yet found a coherent theoretical ground on which to conduct their work of reevaluating cultural traditions in light of environmental concerns. And most scientists remain dualists operating from assumptions that place humans above or outside the biological community that is the object of their empirical study. Environmentalist discourse in many fields remains trapped in dualistic thinking, unconsciously perpetuating the Emersonian distinctions of the human "Me" and the nonhuman "Not Me" even as it advocates a "return" to some primordial relation to "Nature" of the kind Ionesco imagined.

As Val Plumwood has made clear, deep ecology is not the antidote, for it seeks to escape from anthropocentric individualism and dualism by positing an equally egotistical expanded self that absorbs and flattens all of nature in its attempt to identify indiscriminately with the biosphere. Plumwood urges instead a relational account of the self "which clearly recognizes the distinctness of nature but also our relationship and continuity with it" and which acknowledges the ways in which anthropocentrism and androcentrism have been linked.[3] Such a relational account has been under way since the early decades of the twentieth century among phenomenologists such as Martin Heidegger, Maurice Merleau-Ponty, and Emmanuel Levinas. In fact, some commentators include Derrida himself in this

Introduction

company, even though he rejected what he saw as phenomenology's central "metaphysics of presence."[4]

This book shows that Merleau-Ponty was moving to answer the questions about human relations with the rest of nature more broadly than were these other philosophers, and well before the end of the twentieth century, when Derrida addressed them. I write as an environmental literary critic, not as a professional philosopher, with the purpose of introducing Merleau-Ponty's thought to environmental humanists, providing an ecocritical consideration of his philosophy of nature as it anticipates present debates in critical animal studies and understands literature and the other human arts as part of a continuum of meaningful communications and aesthetic behaviors throughout the living world. At each stage in the process, I examine literary works that explore the same issues in dynamic modes inaccessible to discursive theory and science. As Susan McHugh tells us in *Animal Stories: Narrating across Species Lines*, "story forms operate centrally within shifting perceptions of species life" and "concern the very conditions of possibility for human (always with other) ways of being."[5]

Merleau-Ponty insisted early in his career that "the only *Logos* that pre-exists is the world itself";[6] he developed this notion further in his late *Nature* lectures to claim that "animality is the logos of the sensible world: an incorporated meaning."[7] Thus human language and aesthetic behaviors emerge from our animality. In his final working note, written only a few months before his death, he said that he wanted to show that "we can no longer think according to this cleavage: God, man, creatures," but instead must describe nature as "the man-animality *intertwining*." Logos is what is realized in us—our self-conscious understanding of the incorporated meaning of animality, "but nowise is it [our] *property*."[8]

Merleau-Ponty's understanding of human thought and language can provide crucial support and illumination for debates in environmental humanities, critical animal studies, and actual experimental work on cognition and communication among species. His consideration of animals is the focus of attention in this effort because they are obviously closest to us in the realm we call "nature," or "nonhuman" reality, and for him, "Animality and human being are given only together, within a whole of Being that would have been visible ahead of time in the first animal had there been someone to read it" (*N* 271). Here he signals the central importance of evolutionary history for any reevaluation of the human place within the animal community of the biosphere.

In *The Animal That Therefore I Am*, Derrida undermined the long Western philosophical humanist tradition of objectifying "the animal," playfully exposing his own animality and calling for ethical attention to animals as distinct beings. He criticized previous philosophers for ignoring the rich body of scientific animal studies, implying that theoretical claims should be measured against ethological work with real animals in order to have any validity. Yet he adamantly denied any biological continuity between *Homo sapiens* and the rest of organic life, and he himself failed to discuss the findings of modern primatology or other kinds of work on animal cognition or communication. In the 1950s, Merleau-Ponty was already doing what Derrida suggested half a century later. His careful examinations of selected animal studies within an evolutionary perspective in the *Nature* lectures were designed to give a depth to the human body, an archaeology, a natal past, a phylogenetic reference, "to restore it in a fabric of preobjective, enveloping being, from which it emerges and which recalls to us its identity as sensing and sensible at every moment" (*N* 273). The present study extends his efforts by placing his work in dialogue with recent studies of real animals, their cultures and modes of communication. The increasing body of archaeology and scientific studies of animal behavior and cognition shows that humans cannot be considered separate from other living creatures with whom we coevolved and share ancestry, genetic makeup, and morphology. Thus, as Balkan German ethologist Jakob von Uexküll explained with his *Umwelt* theory, we overlap with the others in many ways and can understand them to some degree, as they can us, because of a long shared past and similar physical qualities, abilities, and habits. This is not a question of anthropomorphism. Indeed, as many commentators have pointed out, the charge of anthropomorphism is completely human centered, for it assumes that no other creature could possibly have any of our qualities.[9] We and other creatures observe each other, compete and conflict with each other, and also cooperate or at least live in various sorts of arrangements with each other as we have done for millions of years. Human cultural performance and production, including literature, have reflected these relationships since the earliest records available to us, from Paleolithic cave paintings in France and South Africa to *The Epic of Gilgamesh*.

In a radical challenge to anthropocentric arrogance, Merleau-Ponty's thought restores us to our place in the community of animals and the wider biological community. He called for a radical reinterpretation of Montaigne's "What do I know?" which would include "Where am I?" and "Who am I?" as well as "What is there?" and even "What is the *there is*?" By enacting what he called "an original manner of aiming at something, as it were a *question-knowing*" (*VI* 128–129), his work restores an attitude of openness to the plenitude of the world, urging a questioning which "lets the perceived world be" and before which "the things form and undo themselves in a sort of gliding, beneath the yes and the no" of our desire for positive answers (*VI* 102). Beginning in the 1940s, Merleau-Ponty began developing a philosophy focused on the body and its enmeshment within the dynamic matrix of the biosphere. In *Phenomenology of Perception*, he worked carefully through the traditional dualistic arguments of realism (or reality centered in an objective material world) and idealism (distrust of the material realm of nature and appeal to eternal ideal reality outside ordinary experience) to show how these divisions collapse when philosophical attention returns to "the things themselves" and when the body is taken seriously in its participatory dialogues with the active world around us. No metaphysics of presence is suggested in this long and painstaking examination of embodiment. Merleau-Ponty relied consistently on Gestalt psychology and the neuroscience of his day in making his case, always emphasizing the mediating neural structures of the brain in perception, the destruction of cognitive abilities caused by brain damage, the body's functioning as a limiting situation that determines what we can perceive, and the ways our tools become extensions of our bodies in our interactions with the world. He also took into account individual predispositions and the way ethnicity and personal experience shape perception.

In Merleau-Ponty's later work, he acknowledged the influence of Uexküll's theory of a distinctive *Umwelt* for each organism and individual animal. This he described as the subjective reality created by each organism's dynamic participation in the world around it. The human *Umwelt* is a sort of bubble created by our perceptive abilities and cultural formation in dynamic interchange with our surroundings.[10] By the time of Merleau-Ponty's early death in 1961, he had developed a philosophy that seems obviously ecological today but that no one at the time would have been able to describe in those terms.[11] His project was the redefinition of nature, not centered on humanity as the apex of creation as with Descartes, nor from Spinoza's division into God, man, and creatures, but instead as we have seen earlier, as "a description of the man-animality *intertwining*" (*VI* 274). The unfinished manuscript of a book that would accomplish the first part of his three-part project (The Visible) was posthumously published as *The Visible and the Invisible* in 1968. During the last three years of his life, his lectures at the Collège de France focused on the second topic, Nature. Notes from these lectures were published as *La Nature* in 1968 and 1994 and finally in English translation as *Nature* in 2003. Here he examined the philosophical history of the concept "Nature" as a prelude to moving beyond Descartes to a vision congruent with twentieth-century science. In doing so, he explored the philosophical consequences of quantum physics, evolutionary biology, embryology, and ethology as accompaniment to his overall description of a world of intertwining beings and things within an encompassing flesh full of meaning and wildness which is the ground of human experience. His inquiry includes the geography and history of the planet, the dynamic space/time story of evolution. How the third part of his project (Logos) might have been developed can only be extrapolated from working notes left behind at his death and from comments on the Logos of nature and animality and on language in his other publications.

Merleau-Ponty's thought has become foundational for scholars such as Canadian/British anthropologist Tim Ingold and Danish biochemist/biosemiotician Jesper Hoffmeyer, who seek to link scientific and humanistic understandings of the world with environmental concerns and a coherent synthesis of all levels of recent work in the life sciences. Ingold describes his long professional evolution within anthropology, seeking to move beyond dualism and to find a way to "close the gap between the arts and the humanities on the one hand, and the natural sciences on the other."[12] Merleau-Ponty's philosophy and the late work of James Gibson in ecological psychology helped him to overcome this dualism and to understand that perception is not the achievement of a mind in a body but rather of a whole organism in its exploratory movement through the world. Gibson's concept of the mind as immanent in the network of the organism's sensory activities within its environment were anticipated a generation earlier in Merleau-Ponty's assertion that we ourselves are "this very knot of relations" in a world full of meaning (*PP* lxxxv). In *Biosemiotics: An Examination into the Signs of Life and the Life of Signs*, Hoffmeyer supports key arguments about the meaningful communication of organisms with references to Merleau-Ponty's nondualistic, embodied description of subjectivity, his view of human mental life as predisposed for narrative thinking and organized as a series of "I cans" in purposeful reaching out in interaction with the world, and his theories of language as an extension of those embodied activities (26, 35, 172, 226, 304, 325, 386). Such recent work in fields other than literary and cultural studies indicates how Merleau-Ponty's thought is enabling new ways of thinking about human behaviors and relationships with other organisms.

The discussion that follows consists of three chapters and a conclusion. It moves from an overview of Merleau-Ponty's philosophy and its relation to twentieth-century science to a more particular consideration of animals and animality in the context of recent critical animal theory and scientific studies of actual animals, and finally it focuses on semiotic behavior in animals and humans. Chapter 1, "A Philosophy of Life," introduces Merleau-Ponty's development within the wider project of phenomenology initiated by Edmund Husserl in the early decades of the twentieth century, emphasizing particularly his distinctive focus on the body and his lifelong engagement with modern science. Merleau-Ponty's philosophical theories are surveyed, from his foundational work on embodiment in *Phenomenology of Perception* (1945) to his chiasmic ontology of *The Visible and the Invisible* (1964) that describes humans dynamically intertwined with the things and the organisms in the constantly evolving "Flesh" of the world that is an environment of wild or brute being. Finally I discuss his examination of modern science in the *Nature* lectures presented at the Collège de France during the same period that he was working on *The Visible and the Invisible*. The chapter closes with readings of W. H. Auden's "A New Year Greeting," on the microbial ecosystem living on his skin, and a passage from Eudora Welty's "The Wanderer," both of which offer literary depictions of the embodied nature of human experience defined in Merleau-Ponty's philosophy.

Chapter 2, "Animal Kin," begins by examining the anxiety expressed in two ancient literary works—*The Epic of Gilgamesh* and Euripides's *Bakkhai*—that question human efforts to control the natural world and to separate our species from other animals. These works indicate how such uneasiness goes back to the earliest cultural records we know. Thinking about them as dramatic explorations of human relations with wild creatures casts them in a new light as anguished depictions of the disastrous consequences of refusal to respect our kinship with other animals and the wider biological community in which we are enmeshed.

With such deep cultural history in mind, we turn to examine these concerns in recent animal studies debates, in order to show how Merleau-Ponty's work on the animal question anticipated and even moved beyond the positions of most current commentators in critical animal studies. His investigations of the science of his time move toward the acknowledgment of an evolutionary continuum of humans and other organisms. In contrast to Heidegger, Derrida, and most present commentators, in the *Nature* lectures, Merleau-Ponty explores evolutionary biology, embryology, Uexküll's *Umwelt* theory, and Lorenz and Tinbergen's ethology in ways that anticipate late twentieth-century scientific studies of animal culture and toolmaking.

Chapter 3, "Language Is Everywhere," addresses the place of language and literature in Merleau-Ponty's thought and places it within the context of evolutionary continuity in animal life and the increasing complexity of semiotic behaviors during that long historical unfurling. Merleau-Ponty's linguistic theories in *Phenomenology of Perception, Consciousness and the Acquisition of Language,* and *The Visible and the Invisible* define human language as embodied and gestural, closely related to systems of communication among other organisms. His theories are placed in dialogue with recent studies of the evolution of language, and his analysis of literature and the other arts is explained as it defines their function as the distinctively human manifestation of the sedimentation of experience that underlies all life forms on the planet. The discussion then moves to demonstrate the relevance of his linguistic philosophy to recent animal language studies, particularly with chimpanzees and bonobos such as Kanzi and Panbanisha, and with biosemiotics. Finally Yann Martel's novel *Life of Pi* is discussed as an allegory of conflicted animal kinship and communication in a radically diminished ecosystem.

This study concludes that Merleau-Ponty established a radical new way of understanding the human place in the biosphere, one congruent with twentieth-century science and animal studies. His work finds its place as a crucial theoretical bridge linking disciplines from the humanities to the primarily scientific fields surveyed in Jesper Hoffmeyer's *Biosemiotics*. We see some of the ways that biosemiotics and zoosemiotics can more fully connect with environmental humanism through extensions of Merleau-Ponty's writings on language and culture as manifestations of a meaningful universe.

All along the way, I call attention to the ways Merleau-Ponty integrated his thinking with the sciences of his day, from the beginning of his career until his death. While he criticized positivist claims that objective science could capture all truth, he saw scientists as providing the most carefully regulated attention to nature that our culture achieves. For him, the sciences and philosophy were complementary explorations of the world and thus necessarily engaged in productive dialogue with each other. Glen Love, Dana Phillips, and Greg Garrard have urged ecocritics to familiarize themselves with the sciences that describe the ecological systems on which the planet's life depends.[13] Although this is a daunting challenge, intelligent books have been written by distinguished scientists for lay readers throughout the past century. Earlier generations of writers and thinkers made use of such works, and we can do it too. Virginia Woolf read popular explanations of relativity theory and quantum mechanics by Arthur Eddington and James Jeans, just as Merleau-Ponty did around the same time. In our day, scientists from Stephen J. Gould and Carl Sagan to Stephen Hawking, Richard Dawkins, Lynn Margulis, Jane Goodall, Frans de Waal, Antonio Demasio, and many, many others provide access to major advances in physics, cosmology, evolutionary biology, archaeology, ethology, cognitive neuroscience, and many ecological sciences. As Merleau-Ponty availed himself of scientific writing in these fields from the 1920s through the 1950s, so the present study engages recent work in many of these areas to demonstrate how his thinking anticipated important discoveries that bear on the fate of our species within the wider natural world.

We will share the fate of the earth with the other creatures and plants. Already in 1988 James Lovelock wrote, "The present frenzy of agriculture and forestry is a global ecocide as foolish as it would be to act on the notion that our brains are supreme and the cells of other organs expendable. Would we drill wells through our skins to take the blood for its nutrients?"[14] Lovelock's attitude has darkened in the intervening years as he has watched continued denial of environmental problems by governmental and corporate organizations and enormous increases in fossil fuel use, pollution, and destructive industrial practices. He recently asserted that global disaster is now unavoidable: "I think we have little option but to prepare for the worst and assume that we have already passed the threshold. . . . We face unrestrained heat, and its consequences will be with us within no more than a few decades. We should now be preparing for a rise of sea level, spells of near-intolerable heat like that in Central Europe in 2003, and storms of unprecedented severity."[15] Most of the earth will be covered by desert, and the few animal and plant survivors will gather at the poles to live. Human civilization will have disappeared (*Revenge of Gaia* xiv). If Lovelock is right, we had better learn to live more cooperatively with other creatures; we will all have to survive together in small, threatened numbers.

But even if Lovelock is wrong, that same kind of reengagement with our animal kin, and indeed with all living communities, will be absolutely required for mitigation of the changes we see already beginning. Literature, philosophy, and the arts are our way of talking with ourselves and the world, in an exploration of mysteries we cannot name but can only call to witness by imaginative projection, by the creation of wild possibilities, by reaching into the Invisible. If Merleau-Ponty is right about how art and literature work, then we will learn to sing the world in a new way, participating with the emergence of the future, in common with all our animal kin. Timothy Morton exhorts us to realize that "the ecological thought" is the thinking of interconnectedness (*Ecological Thought* 7). But Merleau-Ponty had already expounded it in careful detail half a century earlier. Thinking along with his philosophy can help us recover our ancient ancestors' awareness that the world is full of meaning, and we can make a bridge with biosemiotics and zoosemiotics to cooperative and complementary relations between the humanistic and scientific disciplines that only together can shape a new, much fuller understanding of the world we share with all other organisms. As Jean-Christophe Bailly warns in *The Animal Side*, his haunting meditation on the ubiquitous and mysterious presence of animals in human thought, if we do not reawaken a keen sense of our originary relations with these companions, we may lose their necessary presence around us.[16]

CHAPTER

1

A Philosophy of Life

Human beings and their cultures are deeply enmeshed in the coevolutionary history of life forms, as well as being dynamically involved with the nonliving forms, materials, and energies of the world. But most of Western philosophical tradition has defined humans in dualistic terms as essentially *outside* of nature, functioning as disembodied minds with access to timeless spiritual realms. As philosopher Mark Johnson puts it, "Although most people never think about it very carefully, they live their lives assuming and acting according to a set of dichotomies that distinguish mind from body, reason from emotion, and thought from feeling."[1] Johnson locates the source of such mistaken assumptions in the way embodied thinking is hidden from our normal awareness, so that we have the illusion that our minds are separate from our bodies. Whatever the physiological cause, this way of thinking is an ancient pattern that is clearly expressed in Plato's works, in Christian theology, in humanist proclamations of the Italian Renaissance, and most systematically in the mechanistic philosophy of Descartes, which until the late nineteenth century dominated the intellectual life of our culture.

Perhaps as part of a reaction against Enlightenment reason and the blight of industrial cities, a fascination with the animal world and the planet's history gave birth to a wave of new life sciences in the nineteenth century, among which Charles Darwin's work was a climactic breakthrough. In a sense, everyone in Western intellectual life has been a Darwinian since the ideas published in the *Origin of Species* and *The Descent of Man* began to overwhelm resistance in the last decades of the nineteenth century. But at the same time, modern urban life and its increasing technological sophistication have allowed popular culture and much of intellectual life to continue assuming Enlightenment concepts about human superiority to all other life and essential separation from it. But the deepening sense of environmental crisis brought by widespread extinctions, melting glaciers, droughts, and extreme weather events associated with global climate change makes these contradictory assumptions increasingly impossible to sustain. Phenomenology, and particularly the work of Maurice Merleau-Ponty, moves beyond this confusion, offering a coherent theoretical grounding for environmentally oriented perspectives on culture and particularly for ecocriticism with its attention to literature's exploration of the human place in the natural world. Merleau-Ponty is the only major European philosopher who embraces the consequences of evolution and sees humans as interdependent members of the ecosystem. His thinking manifests a lifelong engagement with modern science, which he saw in a necessary complementarity with philosophy. Although his untimely death prevented the completion of his ambitious project, enough of the work in progress exists in manuscript to indicate its shape and importance as a radically ecological philosophy.

Because phenomenology was developed by Edmund Husserl early in the twentieth century in reaction to a European philosophical tradition which seemed to have reached a dead end, at the outset we should briefly sketch the specific terms by which that tradition has defined the human place in the natural world. Pico della Mirandola provided one of the most extreme formulations of humanism in his *Oration on the Dignity of Man* of 1486. There he described man as an amphibian who can move at will up and down the hierarchy of nature, with the power to transcend the flesh, the earth, and even the position of the angels. As a free and proud agent, a human being can shape his or her own being, descending "to the lower, brutish forms of life" or rising to the superior, divine orders as "a pure contemplator, unmindful of the body, wholly withdrawn into the chambers of the mind, . . . [neither a creature] of earth nor a heavenly creature, but some higher divinity, clothed with human flesh."[2]

Pico's vision became systematized during the scientific revolution that began in the seventeenth century. In England, Francis Bacon transformed such tendencies into what Carolyn Merchant describes as a program advocating total control of nature for human benefit through science. In France, René Descartes and his fellow rationalists Marin Mersenne and Pierre Gassendi introduced a mechanistic view of the world "as an antidote to intellectual uncertainty and as a new rational basis for social stability," according to Merchant.[3] Descartes determined never to accept anything as true that was not certain and evident in his mind, and therefore he believed that doubting was the same as ignorance. In order to attain certainty, he insisted that only simple problems with clear solutions should be explored, and from those solutions one could move by degrees to composite knowledge.[4] Because our senses often mislead us, he decided that they could not lead to certainty. Instead he relied on Mind as a disembodied essence outside an essentially inert, mechanical Nature, and this *Cogito* links our species with the divine order through the clear language of mathematics. The first truth that struck him with certainty was his famous declaration, "I think, therefore I am," which he made the first principle of his philosophy (51) and which he extended to humans in general. Our whole essence or nature is to think and is something which, in order to exist, "does not have need of any place, and does not depend on any material thing" (53). In contrast to humans, animals "do not have any mind at all, and . . . it is nature that acts in them according to the disposition of their organs," Descartes explained, "just as one sees that a clock, which is composed only of wheels and of springs," can register accurate time (83). Isaac Newton fully realized the kind of vision Descartes espoused by providing what Merchant calls "the most powerful synthesis of the new mathematical philosophy" in his *Principia Mathematica* of 1687, thus epitomizing the "dead world resulting from mechanism" (276). As we can see in retrospect, the Cartesian-Newtonian picture of human existence outside a mechanistic, static natural world prevailed for at least two hundred years but began to erode as late nineteenth-century scientific discoveries in biology, geology, and even physics gradually undermined its premises.

Phenomenology was born during the collapse of Cartesian science under the challenge of the New Physics early in the twentieth century, during the same general period that saw the gradual emergence of evolutionary biology in the work of such scientists as Ernst Haekel, Jakob von Uexküll, J. B. S. Haldane, and Theodosius Dobzhansky. Phenomenologists sought a radical new way of doing philosophy, not trapped in any tradition or a priori metaphysical premises such as those of Kant, Hegel, or the positivists. Explicitly initiated as a coherent program by Edmund Husserl, phenomenology was a radical return to "*concrete*, lived human experience in all its richness"[5] and away from the long Western tradition of idealism and skepticism about the reality of the external world. Husserl's followers Martin Heidegger and Maurice Merleau-Ponty extended his thinking into the immanent richness of everyday life and the profound consequences of embodiment within the dynamic life of the earth. Merleau-Ponty describes the experience of discovering phenomenology in terms that aptly describe its value for environmentalists, for it is less an encounter with a new philosophy than it is a recognition of what we have been waiting for (*PP* lxxi).

Three overlapping generations are represented in this turning of Western philosophy: Husserl, who lived from 1859 to 1938 and was Heidegger's mentor and friend; Heidegger, born in 1889 and living until 1976; and Merleau-Ponty, born in 1908 but living only until 1961. Their work opened a new direction for Western philosophy, and it provides a crucial grounding for ecological thought. Husserl and his followers believed that the proper approach to thinking was to describe phenomena instead of trying to capture truth in abstract logical systems. Phenomenology also rejected the Cartesian objectivist position assumed in classical scientific practice, and the naive positivism (or naturalism) based on it, that places human subjects outside or above a material world whose mechanical operations they can precisely describe. As Merleau-Ponty explains in *Phenomenology of Perception*, phenomenology seeks to define a middle ground between the dualistic extremes of intellectualism (idealism) and empiricism (realism) or, in other words, to join "extreme subjectivism with an extreme objectivism through its concept of the world or of rationality" (lxxxiv). In postmodern terms, such a position between extreme constructivism and naïve assertions of direct access to reality means that practical experience in the natural world is mediated by human perceptual abilities and culture but can be described in provisional ways by modern scientific disciplines. Phenomenology approached such a theoretical basis in Merleau-Ponty's late work, in which he sought to establish a theoretical grounding in biology and ethology, as we shall see in the next chapter. "Merleau-Ponty wants always to emphasize the particularities of the relations to the world of different kinds of organisms, their specific kinds of embodiment, and their different environments" (Moran 417). Because Merleau-Ponty extended phenomenological thought in ways which anticipated concerns and discoveries of the life sciences of our own day, Renaud Barbaras says that his ontology deserves a place beyond Husserl and Heidegger, where "phenomenology can read its own future."[6] Before directly engaging Merleau-Ponty's thinking, it will help to suggest how his work moves beyond Husserl's and Heidegger's.

Edmund Husserl urged a refocusing of philosophical attention on ordinary lived experience, which he called the *Lebenswelt*, or "lifeworld." He described this world as intersubjective, shared with the other beings and things that also experience it (Moran 175–181).[7] Although he called for a concentration on immediate experience, however, he never could abandon the concept of transcendent mind, which made him finally an idealist (Moran 77–78, 168–174). Heidegger and Merleau-Ponty developed Husserl's picture of humans as dynamically engaged in an unfolding temporal reality, and both claim the language of poetry as the proper language for questioning that situation. As Charles Taylor says, "one might claim some preeminence for Heidegger, in that he got there first. In the case of Merleau-Ponty, the breakthrough is plainly built on Heidegger's work."[8] But for all Heidegger's profound radicalism, he remained bound within a deeply European frame of reference and grounded his philosophy on a cultural nostalgia for classical Greece which gives it originary status. This tendency is part of what led some of his critics in the 1930s to find idealism hovering in the background of his work. He was anti-Darwinist,[9] antagonistic to science through most of his career,[10] and a believer in a virtually sacred human superiority and separateness among living creatures. Although Merleau-Ponty continued to think in dialogue with both Husserl's and Heidegger's work throughout his life, he broke away from that kind of hierarchical view. He insisted on taking our existence as bodies seriously, while Heidegger evaded doing so, and that made all the difference. Merleau-Ponty's work is engaged and congruent with twentieth-century science. He assumed that humans coevolved with all other life forms, and he embraced a profound human kinship with animals that Heidegger found appalling, as we shall see in the next chapter. Brute or wild being was for Merleau-Ponty the very ground of human life, as he explained in his final, posthumously published book: "This environment of brute existence and essence is not something mysterious: we never quit it, we have no other environment" (*VI* 116–117).

In order to understand this perspective, we should review the general context for Heidegger's and Merleau-Ponty's work and look more closely at the appeal of Heidegger's philosophy for ecocriticism and at some key problems in Heidegger's definition of the human. We should consider positions Merleau-Ponty shares with Heidegger and finally examine how Merleau-Ponty moved in a new direction that fulfilled Husserl's intention of restoring philosophical attention to things themselves and to the dynamic lifeworld. Such a refutation of traditional subject/object, spirit/matter, mind/body dualisms philosophically restores human beings to the rest of the living community. The dialogic relationships among these philosophers are richly textured and can thus be described from a variety of conceptual perspectives, but their relevance for environmental thinking rests especially on the ways they define the human place in the natural world and philosophy's relation to the life sciences.

Martin Heidegger spent ten years deeply engaged with Husserl's philosophy in an attempt to fulfill his mentor's project of returning to the "things themselves." The result was *Being and Time*, in which he radically questioned what it is to be human in an antidualist, anti-intellectualist examination of how meaning is immanent for us in the ordinary experiences of daily life (Moran 193–194). In this enterprise, Heidegger in some respects was doing for philosophy what modernist novelists such as Marcel Proust, James Joyce, and Virginia Woolf were doing for literature. The minutiae of Leopold Bloom's consciousness of moving through Dublin on June 16, 1904, or of Marcel's experience of lying in bed as a boy, waiting for his mother to come up the stairs, or of Clarissa Dalloway's complex awareness throughout a June day in London soon after World War I—all of these literary revelations of meaning, or what Joyce called epiphanies, attend to similar phenomena as those Heidegger sought to examine. He saw his work as the development of a phenomenological ontology that examined the question of Being, defining human existence with the term *Dasein* to indicate how Being comes into presence for us through language and self-consciousness.

After the turmoil of World War II and the political difficulties resulting from his involvement with National Socialism, Heidegger began to concentrate on the concept of human dwelling on the earth as a way to articulate the distinctively human relation to Being that he had formulated as *Dasein*. In 1951, he asked, "What is the state of dwelling in our precarious age?"[11] In a group of lectures composed around this time, he sought in the figures of myth and poetry some "saving power" that would lead to a new way of understanding humanity's position in an age of technology. As Axel Goodbody remarks, in Heidegger's later works, he "transferred to poetry the hopes he had once notoriously placed in the regeneration of society by National Socialism."[12] He was concerned with many of the questions that trouble us today, such as the modern sense of homelessness, the quality of our being in relation to the planet and the cosmos (earth and sky), and the need for humans to care for the earth and respect its spaces, denizens, and things. He lamented the collapsing of distances caused by airplane travel, the draining out and flattening of experience by television, and the loss of rootedness in earthly life brought by space travel. Many environmental philosophers and literary scholars have found this thinking suggestive of hopeful grounds for a new, environmentally responsible consciousness.

Jonathan Bate's final chapter in *The Song of the Earth* offers Heidegger's late philosophy as an ecopoetics, wherein literature grounds human beings and allows them to save the earth.[13] The poet discloses the being of entities and, in this sacred action, lets them be most fully themselves (Bate 258); Bate defines poetic dwelling as the distinctive way human beings inhabit the earth. Other writers such as poet Martin Harrison and philosopher Michael Zimmerman have also found Heidegger a central thinker for the emerging ecological consciousness. But Heidegger's involvement with National Socialism and reactionary German modernism eventually led Zimmerman to question the degree to which his philosophy offers an adequate understanding of the human place in the world and poetry's ecological possibilities.[14] Bate also raises the question of Heidegger's political past but sidesteps its consequences by recourse to Paul Celan's poem about a disappointing visit with the philosopher for which the sight of the healing plant arnica offered some comfort (268–273). Celan had lost both his parents in a Nazi internment camp and wanted to confront Heidegger on his Nazi past. Although Heidegger apparently remained silent on the subject, Bate suggests that the poem's opening images of the arnica blossom "have connotations of healing, of the possibility of some soothing of the bruise of the Holocaust" (270). Greg Garrard acknowledges the ecocritical importance of Heidegger's emphasis on harmonious dwelling but admits that it has an unfortunate association with the reactionary and xenophobic "blood and soil" enthusiasms of

National Socialism (*Ecocriticism* 111–113). More recently, Garrard has come to a more extreme position, dismissing Heidegger's "views on ontology, technology, history, and poetry" in order to show "that what is distinctive in Heidegger's work after *Being and Time* (1927) is wrong, and what is persuasive is not distinctive" ("Heidegger Nazism Ecocriticism" 251).

Putting aside the controversy over Heidegger's Nazi associations, which will never be fully resolved, we can find in his examination of human dwelling on the earth concerns that motivated late nineteenth-century opponents of industrialism, such as John Ruskin and William Morris, and that seem even more pressing today. But a closer look at his essays from the late 1940s and early 1950s, such as "Letter on Humanism" (1947), "Building, Dwelling, Thinking" (1951), and "The Question Concerning Technology" (1953), in which the concept of careful dwelling is developed, reveals a troubling humanistic elitism. Heidegger grants sentience and agency *only* to humans. For him, humans are not animals. Rather, they are closer to the "divine" than they are to other animals in the fourfold "unity" of divinities, mortals, earth, and sky. For Heidegger, man dwells poetically, but "dwelling" means not only carefully letting things be to realize their essences but also building and thinking, shaping the things that create meaningful locations in space. Only men and women (and only *some* of them) can dwell properly so that Being comes into presence for them. That is because *Dasein* is by definition only possible for humans who have a full awareness of their movement toward death. It results from a kind of self-consciousness made possible by language. As he explained in "Letter on Humanism," "What man is—or, as it is called in the traditional language of metaphysics, the 'essence' of man—lies in his ek-sistence." This means that "man occurs essentially in such a way that he is the 'there' (*das, 'Da'*), that is, the lighting of Being. The 'Being' of the *Da*, and only it, has the fundamental character of 'ek-sistence,' that is, of an ecstatic inherence in the truth of Being."[15]

Given this essentially separate status which seems to reinstate traditional mind/body dualism, Heidegger's view of human destiny suggests the kind of dominance assumed in humanism. It is clearly implied in his distinctive concept of dwelling set forth in "Building, Dwelling, Thinking." Human dwelling means acting on the world, as Heidegger explains in a complicated argument based on German etymology. Delving into the Old High German backgrounds of the verb *bauen*, "to build," he claims that its archaic meaning was derived from *bin*, "to be," and synonymous with the concept of dwelling, "to remain, to stay in place." Thus,

> The way in which you are and I am, the manner in which we humans *are* on the earth, is *buan*, dwelling. To be a human being means to be on the earth as a mortal. It means to dwell. The old word *bauen*, which says that man *is* insofar as he *dwells*, this word *bauen*, however, *also* means at the same time to cherish and protect, to preserve and care for, specifically to till the soil, to cultivate the vine. Such building only takes care—it tends the growth that ripens into its fruit of its own accord. Building in the sense of preserving and nurturing is not making anything. [*But he goes on to include the constructing of things such as ships and houses also as "comprised within genuine building"*].[16]

From a practical ecological perspective, this position fails to acknowledge the historical evolution of agriculture as involving the manipulation of wild plants to make them serve human purposes, and the tilling of the soil, which disrupts the normal diversity of microorganisms and patterns of water retention and plant diversity. Extending this consideration to animal husbandry and recent advances in genetic engineering makes the violent invasiveness of such activities obvious in ways Heidegger was unlikely to anticipate. Vandana Shiva's *Staying Alive* offers an extreme example of how industrial agriculture has destroyed the soils of India.[17] Although Heidegger's concept of dwelling has proved attractive to ecocritics and environmental theorists in its positive sense of human interrelationship with plants and the soil, his argument also suffers from being grounded in the linguistic contingency of one particular European community.

In a passage describing the function of a bridge as exemplary of building, we see very clearly how in Heidegger's view, dwelling means building structures that are required for place to have meaning. He writes about the bridge as if from outside the scene, playing what Donna Haraway calls "the god trick," of seeing from everywhere and nowhere, not from any situation within the world.[18]

> The bridge swings over the stream "with ease and power." It does not just connect banks that are already there. The banks emerge as banks only as the bridge crosses the stream. The bridge designedly causes them to lie across from each other. . . . The bridge *gathers* the earth as landscape around the stream. Thus it guides and attends the stream through the meadows. . . . Even where the bridge covers the stream, it holds its flow up to the sky by taking it for a moment under the vaulted gateway and then setting it free once more. . . . The bridge *gathers* to itself in *its own* way earth and sky, divinities and mortals. . . . Thus the bridge does not first come to a location to stand in it; rather a location comes into existence only by virtue of the bridge. ("Building, Dwelling, Thinking" 330–332)

For Heidegger, therefore, building is a human intervention in nature, a shaping dwelling into which he subjectively projects enormous agency, apparently from outside the normal workings of the natural world. No place on earth seems to have meaning without the presence of human structures; for beaver or deer, there are neither banks for the river nor significant locations along it. Human buildings are required in order to gather the "fourfold unity" of Being and to care for the world.[19]

Recently, Kate Rigby has sought to rehabilitate Heidegger's concept of dwelling in an elegant reinterpretation of the fourfold of earth, sky, divinities, and mortals, so that it sounds less archaic and mystical than Heidegger's original formulation.

> The fourfold comprises earth, understood as the land itself with its particular topography, waterways, and biotic community; sky, including the alternation of night and day, the rhythm of the seasons, and the vagaries of the weather; divinities, those emissaries or traces that yet remain of an absent God; and, last but not least, mortals, fellow humans, those who, in Heidegger's (questionable) view, alone know that they will die.[20]

She sees poetry as the human way of singing the world, in concert with all the other voices of the biota. With such an adaptation of Heidegger's conception of poetry, like Jonathan Bate before her, she extends a kind of worlding and lighting of Being to other creatures and thus erases the distinctively human way of bringing truth into presence. However, it is hard to imagine how Heidegger could have accepted a reshaping of his vision of the world to remove the separate role he saw for human beings.

Heidegger's repeated insistence on the unique status of humans as shepherds of Being, essentially distinct from the rest of creation, seems to me a disabling flaw in the usefulness of his philosophy for ecocriticism. This is the kind of hubris that David Ehrenfeld blamed for the present environmental crisis, in *The Arrogance of Humanism*.[21] While there is no doubt that our species has an enormous impact on the global environment and corresponding responsibilities for restraining or mitigating that impact, Heidegger's claims of human uniqueness are logically incompatible with evolutionary biology, cognitive neuroscience, and the past century's work in physics. When, exactly, did humans diverge from their coevolved living kin and become capable of *Dasein*? With Lucy, *Homo habilis*, or the fossil finds and Paleolithic cave art from the south of France to South Africa? Or during the Neolithic period, when they began to manipulate plant and animal reproduction and build megaliths such as Newgrange and Stonehenge? For that matter, when does an individual human person become capable of *Dasein*? At age three or so, when language is acquired, or later, when complex reasoning is possible? Is the capacity for *Dasein* located in the cerebral cortex only? How is it related to the limbic system? What happens when brain lesions result from wounds or illness, and particular mental capacities are lost? As we shall see in the next chapter, Heidegger refused to consider evolution seriously and resisted any notion of human animality, whereas Merleau-Ponty pondered it carefully during the last years of his life and was moving toward the new understandings of animal intelligence and agency revealed by the recent flurry of animal studies in our own time.

Merleau-Ponty received a different philosophical education than Heidegger, though each was deeply marked by the sacramental attitudes of a Catholic upbringing that shaped his orientation toward the natural world. Whereas Heidegger moved through a German academic training in Catholic and then Protestant theology to work directly with Edmund Husserl, Merleau-Ponty was trained in a rather conservative French philosophical tradition and only came to phenomenology informally through conversations and explorations with his friends, especially Jean-Paul Sartre. In an essay called "The Philosophy of Existence," he described the philosophical milieu in which his generation developed in France. He explained that during the 1920s, Henri Bergson's influence was waning while a neo-Kantian idealism dominated philosophical training. But during the 1930s, he and his friends discovered Husserl, Jaspers, Heidegger, and Gabriel Marcel—the philosophers of existence who emphasized "a completely different theme, that of *incarnation*." Instead of considering the body as an object, as Western philosophy had done since the Greeks, these philosophers began to realize that we are given our experiences through our flesh, and therefore we need to examine "this sensible and carnal presence of the world."[22] The new philosophy of existence initiated by Husserl was not only a theme, Merleau-Ponty explained, but really a new style of philosophizing that explored mysteries rather than attempting to analyze clearly defined problems. In this new mode, the philosopher "is not a spectator in relation to the problem, but is rather caught up in the matter, which for him defines the mystery" (133).

Heidegger's attention to Being became the dominant focus among these "philosophers of existence," but during the 1930s, Merleau-Ponty's interest in the body as the source of the experience of Being led him to diverge from Sartre and his other contemporaries. In his postgraduate research, he explored the nature of perception and turned to Gestalt psychology for a holistic tradition that avoided the mechanistic accounts of the behaviorists, on the one hand, and the vitalism of the Bergsonians, on the other. During this period, he was alienated from the Catholic Church's support for violent dictators and after a religious crisis began to investigate Marxist thought as a phenomenology of practical social life (Moran 393).

In Merleau-Ponty's doctoral work at the École Normale Supérieure, he moved from early assumptions about human superiority to the rest of nature (his preliminary thesis, published in 1942: *The Structure of Behavior*) to an exhaustive examination of the body and its evidence for human immersion in the natural world (his major doctoral thesis, published in 1945: *Phenomenology of Perception*). During the 1950s, he developed a philosophy of wild being in which all creatures and things are chiasmically intertwined. Simultaneously he was exploring the philosophical implications of modern physics, evolutionary biology, and ethology in lectures at the Collège de France. These projects were unfinished at his death but resulted in posthumous publications: *The Visible and the Invisible* (in French, 1964; in English, 1968) and *Nature* (in French, 1994; in English, 2003).

Merleau-Ponty's philosophy assumes the evolution of life forms and sees humans as interdependent members of the ecosystem. He argued that each human—like any other organism—exists in an embrace or intertwining with the surrounding environment. He gave this relationship the name *chiasm*, which he took from the Greek *chiasmos*, meaning a diagonal crossing as in the letter *X* or in the DNA molecule. All organisms exist intertwined and in constant interaction with the flesh of the world around them, which is the wild or brute being in which we are immersed. He explained, "This environment of brute existence and essence is not something mysterious: we never quit it, we have no other environment" (*VI* 116–117). Such an ontology is congruent with the sciences, which revolutionized the understanding of the natural world in the twentieth century and whose philosophical ramifications Merleau-Ponty was considering at the end of his life. Though he did not live long enough to know the genetic and molecular discoveries which would demonstrate a common heritage and sharing of genetic material for all organisms, his late philosophy anticipated it. His concept of the flesh of the world and description of its dynamic unfolding through geologic time accords with Lynn Margulis's recent assertion that "all beings alive today are equally evolved. All have survived over three thousand million years of evolution from common bacterial ancestors. There are no 'higher' beings, no 'lower animals,' no angels and no gods."[23] We share the same fate as equal participants in the biota, with its dense ecological texture of interdependence. Derrida's late writings about animality are congruent with much of Merleau-Ponty's thought and extend its concerns into recent studies of animal sentience and culture, as we shall see more specifically in the next chapter.

Merleau-Ponty maintained a lifelong conversation with science from an appreciative yet critical distance. In the preface to *Phenomenology of Perception*, in which he seeks to define phenomenology and to place his own enterprise in the context of Husserl's and Heidegger's work, he defines uncritical scientific points of view as "always naïve and hypocritical because they always imply, without mentioning it, that other perspective—the perspective of consciousness—by which a world first arranges itself round me and begins to exist for me." Phenomenology seeks to return to the things themselves, which is "to return to this world prior to knowledge, this world of which knowledge always *speaks*, and this world with regard to which every scientific determination is abstract, signitive, and dependent, just like geography with regard to the landscape where we first learned what a forest, a meadow, or a river is" (lxxii).

For him, "classical science is a perception that has forgotten its origins and believes itself to be complete" (*PP* 57). Nevertheless, Merleau-Ponty's work was consistently engaged with the science of his day, particularly with Gestalt psychology and the disciplines of neuroscience during the 1930s and 1940s and with physics, animal studies, human physiology, and evolutionary biology in the 1950s. His philosophical descriptions of perception and embodiment were deeply informed by scientific experimentation, and his late work explored the philosophical dimensions of the major fields of twentieth-century science.

There is no contradiction between Merleau-Ponty's insistence on recognizing the limitations of scientific knowledge and his lifelong interdisciplinary involvement with its major disciplines. He valued the careful attention to nature that science alone provides, while at the same time his critical distance enabled his style of phenomenology to complement scientific findings by identifying their limitations and placing them within a larger, more complex frame of interpretation. Near the end of his life, he was reflecting explicitly on the relationship of philosophy to science. In his course "The Concept of Nature" in 1956–1957, he confronted the relationship of science and philosophy, calling science "a naïve and uncritical enjoyment of the natural certitude" which "still lives in part on a Cartesian myth" of certainty about "nature as an object spread out in front of us." But he explains that much science of his own time was self-critical, placing "its own object and its relation to this object in question" (*N* 85).

Because of the indeterminacy resulting from relativity theory and quantum mechanics, the thinking of many modern physicists was tentative in ways unthinkable for classical Newtonian mechanics, as Merleau-Ponty explains in his lectures titled "Classical and Modern Physics" (*N* 88–100). By the middle of the twentieth century, scientists in many fields were aware of the contingency of their work, and in general he believed that the point had been reached at which "we cannot think Nature without taking account to ourselves that our idea of Nature is impregnated with artifice" (*N* 86).

Such an understanding is paralleled by attention to contingency and relativism in modernist painting and fiction, and Merleau-Ponty's work also considers relations between philosophy and the arts similarly to the way he describes the necessary cooperation between philosophy and science.

> The concern of the philosopher is to see; that of the scientist is to find a foothold. His thinking is directed by the concern not of seeing but of intervening. He wants to escape getting bogged down in the philosophical way of looking at things. Does he also often work like a blind man by analogy? Did a solution work out for him? He tries it on something else, because that time it was successful. The scientist has the superstition of means that succeed. But in this attempt to get a firm grip on things, the scientist discloses more than he sees in fact. *The philosopher must see behind the back of the physicist what the physicist himself does not see.* . . .
> How thus not to be interested in science in order to know what Nature is? If Nature is an all-encompassing something we cannot think starting from concepts, let alone deductions, but we must rather think it starting from experience, and in particular, experience in its most regulated form—that is, science. (*N* 86–87)

Merleau-Ponty intended to explain more systematically how the philosopher "sees behind" the scientist and helps to show the larger dynamic whole within which each scientific project exists. One of the working notes left behind at his death was a direction to himself dated January 4, 1960, to "justify science as an operation within the given situation of knowledge—and thereby make apparent the necessity of the ontology 'complementarity' with this operational science— . . . *By principle* science is not an *exhausting*, but a physiognomic portrait" of features of the world (*VI* 225). Clearly, for him science was a privileged site for the experience of nature, but its description of that experience is radically limited by its reductionist methods and partial access to a reality which can never be fully captured by observers from within its very texture.

Conceptual/political struggles within the biological sciences at present demonstrate that many researchers continue to assume the Cartesian mechanistic paradigm, while others contest its reductionist premises along the lines that Merleau-Ponty suggested. Biologist Steven Rose speaks of his discipline in terms that echo Merleau-Ponty's concerns. He explains that biologists need an epistemological pluralism to approach "the radical indeterminacy of living processes." Such indeterminacy "is not merely a matter of ignorance, or lack of adequate technology; it is inherent in the nature of life itself."[24] As Bruno Latour points out in *We Have Never Been Modern*, the history of modern science begins with the development of the laboratory, which can drastically reduce this indeterminacy.[25] Rose reminds us that such simplification comes at a price.

> Effective experiments demand the artificial controls imposed by the reductive methodology of the experimenter, but we must never forget that as a consequence they provide only a very simplified model, perhaps even a false one, of what happens in the blooming, buzzing, interactive confusion of life at large, where things rather rarely happen one at a time and snakes intervene inconveniently. (28)

Biologists such as E. O. Wilson and Richard Dawkins continue to rely on simplified mechanistic explanations for living processes that others such as Rose and Richard Lewontin describe as far more complex. "Ultra-Darwinism," as Rose terms the reductionist approach, is a sort of Hobbesian vision of ruthless struggle for reproductive success and adaptation at the level of what Dawkins calls "the selfish gene" that renders organisms mere robots. Dawkins goes so far as to claim, "We are built as gene machines, . . . but we have the power to turn against our creators. We, alone on earth, can rebel against the tyranny of the selfish replicators."[26] Rose exposes the dualism of such a model and explains that it leaves no room for the processes of development, for the internal physiological processes of the organism, or for the organism's agency in shaping its own destiny (214–215). Richard Lewontin, like Rose, urges biologists to move beyond a mechanistic focus on genes and to acknowledge the dynamism and complexity of organisms in their interactions with their environments.

> Everybody "knows" at some level of consciousness that DNA is not self-reproducing, that the information in DNA sequences is insufficient to specify even a folded protein, not to speak of an entire organism, that the environment of an organism is constructed and constantly altered by the life activities of the organism. But this in-principle knowledge cannot become folded into the structure of biological explanation unless it can be incorporated into the actual work of biologists.[27]

Merleau-Ponty's late work sought to explain this situation on the basis of an ontology that complemented the work of scientists by defining a nondualistic nature consisting of a flesh that is not only materiality but also "expression, and ideas 'encrusted in the joints' of things, and a Logos rooted in the world" (Ted Toadvine, personal communication, August 27, 2007).

In order to reach this position, Merleau-Ponty began by turning phenomenology to an examination of the body. Such an emphasis is radical in the dualistic tradition of Western philosophy, which has tended to ignore or denigrate body in favor of mind, just as the natural world has been denigrated in favor of a nonmaterial realm of spirit. For Plato, the body was a flawed part of a changeable material world that itself was only a flawed copy of an eternal realm of ideal forms. Descartes saw human essence as Mind, a substance distinct from the material substance of a mechanical world in which our physical bodies and all other living things are mere machines (116, 150–151, 190–191). Essential human existence would therefore not really be part of material nature, although the body obviously is. Merleau-Ponty's close examination of the body is designed to erase that dualism. In the preface to *Phenomenology of Perception*, he announced, "The world is not what I think, but what I live" (lxxx), and meaning is bodily attunement to that world. The body is "a knot of living significations" clinging to its particular experiences as it moves toward its equilibrium (*PP* 148, 153). The body cannot be a thing apart from the perceiver because as one's gaze moves up the arm from the hand that holds a pen, for example, the thickness of the body's horizon stops the progression. As Ted Toadvine explains, "There is an opacity of my body as a desiring being which subjectivity cannot penetrate, just as there is an ecceity and resistance of matter which cannot in principle be comprehended or brought into the circuit of language."[28] Things in the world around us withhold their full being from our perception.

> From my body's point of view, I never see the six sides of a cube as equal, even if it is made of glass, and yet the word "cube" has a sense. . . . When I see [the six sides of the cube], one after the other and according to perspectival appearance, I do not construct the idea of a geometrical plan that would account for these perspectives; rather, the cube is already there in front of me and unveils itself through them. . . . The thing and the world are given with the parts of my body, not through a "natural geometry," but in a living connection comparable, or rather identical, to the living connection that exists among the parts of my body itself. (*PP* 209–211)

The relations between ourselves as sensing bodies and the sensible things in the world are dynamic, "comparable to those between the sleeper and his sleep: sleep arrives when a certain voluntary attitude suddenly receives from outside the very confirmation that it was expecting" (*PP* 219). Furthermore, if the qualities of the things "radiate a certain mode of existence around themselves, if they have a power to enchant, . . . this is because the sensing subject does not posit them as objects, but sympathizes with them, makes them his own and finds in them his momentary law" (*PP* 221).[29]

In spite of this account of the subject's immersion in the world, Merleau-Ponty was criticized for retaining an emphasis on the unitary consciousness of the perceiver in *Phenomenology of Perception.* Thus the Cartesian *cogito* remains. He himself recognized this problem, writing in a working note of July 1959, "The problems posed in *Ph.P.* are insoluble because I start there from the 'consciousness'-'object' distinction" (*VI* 200). These problems he set out to correct in *The Visible and the Invisible.*

In *The Visible and the Invisible*, Merleau-Ponty began developing an ontology in which individual beings are intertwined with the basic stuff, or flesh, of the universe, existing in a kind of reversibility with other beings and things. Unlike what he calls the *kosmotheoros* of traditional philosophy—"a pure look which fixes the things in their temporal and local place and the essences in an invisible heaven, . . . a ray of knowing that would have to arise from nowhere"—each of us is enmeshed within the visible present and is both seeing and seen, touching and touched by the world and the things around us: "[The visible present] stops up my view, that is, time and space extend beyond the visible present, and at the same time they are *behind* it, in depth, in hiding. The visible can thus fill me and occupy me only because I who see it do not see it from the depths of nothingness, but from the midst of itself; I the seer am also visible" (*VI* 113).

Merleau-Ponty used the term *chiasm* for the reversibility within the tissue or flesh that sustains and nourishes all things. He illustrated it with the metaphor of one's two hands both touching each other and touched by each other, showing a kinship between the body's movements and what it touches.

> This can happen only if my hand, while it is felt from within, is also accessible from without, itself tangible, for my other hand, for example, if it takes its place among the things it touches, is in a sense one of them, opens finally upon a tangible being of which it is also a part. Through this crisscrossing within it of the touching and the tangible, its own movements

incorporate themselves into the universe they interrogate, are recorded on the same map as it; the two systems are applied upon one another, as the two halves of an orange. (*VI* 133)

And yet this reversibility is "always imminent and never realized in fact" (*VI* 147), so that there is no coincidence or merging but instead a divergence or "incessant escaping" (*écart*) that prevents the exact superimposition on one another of "the touching of the things by my right hand and the touching of this same right hand by my left hand" (*VI* 148). Similarly the relation of any creature to others within the flesh of the world is never fully realized or identical; this dehiscence or *écart* generates differentiation even as the intertwining of things and creatures ensures their kinship.

> Why would not the synergy exist among different organisms, if it is possible within each? Their landscapes interweave, their actions and their passions fit together exactly: this is possible as soon as we no longer make belongingness to one same "consciousness" the primordial definition of sensibility, and as soon as we rather understand it as the return of the visible upon itself, a carnal adherence of the sentient to the sensed and of the sensed to the sentient. For, as overlapping and fission, identity and difference, it brings to birth a ray of natural light that illuminates all flesh and not only my own. (*VI* 142)

The emphasis is no longer on the *cogito*, the thinking consciousness of the perceiver, as it was in *Phenomenology of Perception*, but rather on the ecological interrelationships of beings that temporarily emerge in particular forms within the flesh of the world and then merge back into its body again.

These relationships carry with them the weight of time and entanglements with space, woven into an Einsteinian fabric of space-time.

> Like the memory screen of the psychoanalysts, the present, the visible counts so much for me and has an absolute prestige for

me only by reason of this immense latent content of the past, the future, and the elsewhere, which it announces and which it conceals....

In short, there is no essence, no idea, that does not adhere to a domain of history and of geography. Not that it is *confined* there and inaccessible to the others, but because, like that of nature, the space or time of culture is not surveyable from above, and because the communication from one constituted culture to another occurs through the wild region wherein they all have originated....We never have before us pure individuals, indivisible glaciers of beings, nor essences without place and without date. Not that they exist elsewhere, beyond our grasp, but because we are experiences, that is, thoughts that feel behind themselves the weight of the space, the time, the very Being they think, and which therefore do not hold under their gaze a serial space and time nor the pure idea of series, but have about themselves a time and a space that exist by piling up, by proliferation, by encroachment, by promiscuity—a perpetual pregnancy, perpetual parturition, generativity and generality, brute essence and brute existence, which are the nodes and antinodes of the same ontological vibration. (*VI* 114–115)

Within this primordial nature or brute being, each developing life is an upsurge of the Flesh of the world, coiling over on itself, which will eventually return to the whole.[30]

Such an account of the natural world and all the beings and things within it is congruent with the complex substance of life—the coevolution and symbiosis and genetic sharing of plants and animals with the stuff of the biotic microcosmos from which the millions of particular species developed. As Lynn Margulis has explained, symbiosis among bacteria was one of the drivers of evolutionary novelty and the development of complex organisms. Such literal, physical intertwining was not necessarily peaceful or beautiful; indeed, it may well have begun as predation (38–49, 89, 99–103). But Merleau-Ponty's description of the promiscuity and enormous, messy vitality of the natural world (ontological vibrations, generativity of brute essences) matches the kind of evolutionary history that biologists are beginning to document and that in fact is continuing in the biotic soup of our own world. Alphonso Lingis, translator of *The Visible and the Invisible*, points out that we humans live in symbiosis with thousands of species of anaerobic bacteria that inhabit our bodies. We also live in external symbiosis with all the other mammals, the birds, the insects, and with "rice, wheat, and corn fields, with berry thickets and vegetable patches, and also with the nitrogen-fixing bacteria in the soil that their rootlets enter into symbiosis with in order to grow and feed the stalk leaves, and seeds or fruit."[31] This chiasmic understanding of the human place in the biota for Merleau-Ponty includes thought and language.

At the same time that Merleau-Ponty was developing the more general ontology of *The Visible and the Invisible*, he was exploring in his courses at the Collège de France the philosophical dimensions of the twentieth-century knowledge of the natural world as provided by the main branches of science. These courses were one facet of a three-part enterprise described in the "Working Notes" found among his papers after his sudden death at the age of fifty-three. In March 1961, two months before he died, he outlined the plan of his work in progress:

I. The Visible
II. Nature
III. Logos

He wrote that the project "must be presented without any compromise with *humanism*, nor moreover with *naturalism*, nor finally with *theology*—Precisely what has to be done is to show that philosophy can no longer think according to this cleavage: God, man, creatures—which was Spinoza's division." Instead he proposed to describe "the man-animality *intertwining*," and it was in his lecture courses from 1956–1960 that he developed Part II of his project, as the book manuscript was shaping Parts I and III. Notes from the courses, primarily taken by students but including some of his own lecture notes, were published as *La Nature* in 1995 and in English as *Nature* in 2003. Though they are sketchy and most are not from his own pen, they offer a crucial glimpse of his explorations of the philosophical implications of classical and modern physics, animality and the study of animal behavior, the animality of the human body, cybernetics, contemporary developments in Darwinism, and such aspects of evolutionary biology as ontogenesis and phylogenesis.

Nature shows how deeply Merleau-Ponty engaged with the advanced sciences of his day, in an effort to redefine the situation of humans within the natural world. Because this work has only become available recently, its significance and articulation with the ontological work of *The Visible and the Invisible* will take some time to evaluate. But already it is clear that the 1956–1957 course on "the concept of Nature" offered a radical philosophical critique of Aristotelian and Cartesian descriptions of the natural world and explored the philosophical consequences of relativity theory and quantum mechanics. Physicists' difficulty in reconciling particle theory with wave theory created an internal critique within their discipline that led Merleau-Ponty to conclude, "The perceived world is in no way an immediate given. The mediation of knowing allows us to retrieve indirectly and in a negative way the perceived world that anterior idealizations had made us forget." But this conception "does not give us an artificial construction of nature" (*N* 100).

The 1957–1958 course "Animality, the Human Body, and the Passage to Culture" assumes the evolutionary relationship of *Homo sapiens* to other creatures and considers the work of ethologists such as Jakob von Uexküll and Konrad Lorenz in the ways it illuminates questions of environmental perception and relationship among species. In particular, Merleau-Ponty examines the implications of Uexküll's notion of the subjective environment or *Umwelt* that each species and individual creates in its reciprocal interaction with the world around it, as determined by its perceptual and motor abilities (*N* 167–178; see Uexküll, *Stroll*). Lorenz's work on animal instinct and imprinting offers another approach to animal modes of reciprocal interactions with the many environments in which they must survive. Together with Uexküll's work and E. S. Russell's study of relations among cells, Lorenz's affirmation that "none of those who have a familiarity with animals would deny them consciousness" sets up for Merleau-Ponty the project of investigating the sentience in other animals: "Is there animal consciousness, and if so, to what extent?" (*N* 199).

"Nature and Logos: The Human Body," the 1959–1960 course, moves on to explore the human place in evolution, defining our species's uniqueness and yet our essential kinship with other animals. Teilhard de Chardin figures prominently in this course because of his philosophical consideration of human evolution, but finally he is defined as a phenomenological idealist (*N* 269). Even so, Teilhard leads Merleau-Ponty to suggest a definition of the "man-animality intertwining" that he had been considering in his own working notes. From Teilhard's description of man's silent, almost imperceptible appearance in evolution, it follows that the relation of animality and humanity is not hierarchical but lateral (*N* 268), closely associated with the relation between the visible and the invisible (*N* 271).

Clearly for Merleau-Ponty the description of nature in these courses was tentative and preliminary. Nevertheless the lectures indicate his progress toward a radical departure from traditional philosophical descriptions of the natural world and the human place within it. Writing before the *Nature* lectures were published, David Abram could already predict that he was moving toward a vision that recognized animal consciousness and the continuity among species while still acknowledging a distinctive way of being for *Homo sapiens*.[32]

For ecocritics, it is especially important to notice how carefully Merleau-Ponty engaged the life sciences and the questions that increasingly concern practitioners of nature writing, the various branches of environmental studies, animal studies, and cultural theory. But literary works from any period or culture can offer insights of startling environmental relevance when approached from Merleau-Ponty's ontological perspective. Particular applications of Merleau-Ponty's thought to literary analysis include the investigation of ecophenomenological descriptions of the world in poetry and fiction; exploration of the relation of literary works to embodiment; close attention to works exploring human-animality intertwining; and new approaches to works of science fiction that offer dramatizations or performative explorations of interrelations between science, the virtual realities of fiction, and theoretical positions shaped by those interrelations. As I have explained previously, Merleau-Ponty's modernist contemporary Virginia Woolf explored many of the same questions of embodiment and human perception of the phenomenal world in her fiction;[33] in chapter 2, I shall suggest that anxiety about human-animality intertwining has been a powerful force in literary works as ancient as *The Epic of Gilgamesh* and Euripides's *Bakkhai*.

For present purposes, however, I want to offer ecophenomenological readings of two brief examples: a description of a meditative baptismal swim from Eudora Welty's "The Wanderers" and W. H. Auden's poem "A New Year Greeting." In Welty's short story, on the evening of the sudden death of Virgie Rainey's mother from a stroke, Virgie walks down from her farm to the Big Black River for solace. Welty, like Woolf, whose fiction she admired, uses her prose to explore consciousness as embodied participation within a dynamic, intertwining community of plants, animals, and nonliving things. Virgie's swim is an epistemological journey into the texture of space-time that Merleau-Ponty defines as "the wild region" wherein all things have originated. Virgie comes to know with her whole body the enormous scope of history lying within primordial nature and dwarfing the temporary coiling up of individual beings and objects. Their reabsorption into the world's flesh occurs in continual metamorphoses such as the death of her mother or the vast geological changes crushing shells and stones as the earth's skin flexes with the movements of earthquake and glacier.

> She stood on the willow bank. It was bright as mid-afternoon in the openness of the water, quiet and peaceful. She took off her clothes and let herself into the river.
> She saw her waist disappear into reflectionless water; it was like walking into sky, some impurity of skies. All was one warmth, air, water, her own body. All seemed one weight, one matter—until as she put down her head and closed her eyes and the light slipped under her lids, she felt this matter a translucent one, the river, herself, the sky all vessels which the sun filled. She began to swim in the river, forcing it gently, as she would wish for gentleness to her body. Her breasts around which she felt the water curving were as sensitive at that moment as the tips of wings must feel to birds, or antennae to insects. She felt the sand, grains intricate as little cogged wheels, minute shells of old seas, and the many dark ribbons of grass and mud touch her and leave her, like suggestions and withdrawals of some bondage that might have been dear now dismembering and losing itself. She moved but like a cloud in skies, aware but only of the nebulous edges of her feeling and the vanishing opacity of her will, the carelessness for the water of the river through which her body had already passed as well as for what was ahead. The bank was all one, where out of the faded September world the little ripening plums started. Memory dappled her like no more than a paler light, which in slight agitations came through the leaves, not darkening her for more than an instant. The iron taste of the old river was sweet to her, though. If she opened her eyes she looked at bluebottles, the skating water-bugs. If she trembled it was at the smoothness of a fish or snake that crossed her knees.[34]

This passage captures the erotic chiasm that Merleau-Ponty defines for the human body with the world, a relation of embrace in which surfaces or boundaries are not frontiers but rather contact surfaces (*VI* 271). The whole of Virgie's skin becomes the organ of her perception of both visible things and invisible rhythms of time, emotion, and memory. Welty intensifies what Merleau-Ponty sees as the natural magic of language "that attracts the other significations into its web, as the body feels the world in feeling itself" (*VI* 118). In spite of Virgie's sense of bodily indeterminacy and merging with the world around her, she remains a separate being that continues to be aware of the otherness of insects, snakes, ribbons of grass, and fragments of ancient shells. Merleau-Ponty's concept of *écart* accounts for the simultaneous kinship and separateness of human and animal, creatures and things, in this moment of Virgie's release from individual grief. His philosophy illuminates the significance of the epiphany Welty has given to Virgie and, through her, to her readers.

Auden's "New Year Greeting" is far different in tone from Welty's lyrical celebration of the body's chiasmic relation to its *Umwelt*. He comically salutes all the tiny creatures for whom his "ectoderm / is as Middle-Earth," but the poem darkens and sharpens as it moves toward a bleak acknowledgment of destructive forces intertwined with creation and flourishing.[35] In greeting the yeasts, bacteria, and viruses who live on his body, he explains,

> For creatures your size I offer
>   a free choice of habitat,
> so settle yourselves in the zone
>   that suits you best, in the pools
> of my pores or the tropical
>   forests of arm-pit and crotch,
> in the deserts of my fore-arms,
>   or the cool woods of my scalp.

After an invitation to build colonies and enjoy the warmth and nourishment his body supplies, however, he cautions his tiny symbiotic intimates against creating annoyances such as acne or boils. This negative turn intensifies as the poem considers disasters caused by ordinary human movement. Taking a shower broils and drowns millions; changes of clothing bring hurricanes.

> Then, sooner or later, will dawn
>   a day of Apocalypse,
> when my mantle suddenly turns
>   too cold, too rancid, for you,
> appetising to predators
>   of a fiercer sort, and I
> am stripped of excuse and nimbus,
>   a Past, subject to Judgement.

Here is a teasing, intimate meditation on human-animality intertwining that cheerily and sardonically undercuts the godlike anthropocentric illusions of its opening largess. Human exceptionalism is nibbled away as the conscious individual disappears back into the mass of pullulating life forms that Merleau-Ponty describes as the "perpetual pregnancy, perpetual parturition, generativity and generality, brute essence and brute existence, which are the nodes and antinodes of the same ontological vibration" (*VI* 114–115). Like Merleau-Ponty, Auden read science all his life and incorporated it into his writing. This poem was inspired by a 1969 *Scientific American* article about the myriad of tiny symbionts living on and in our bodies, and he turned it into a whimsical musing about the simultaneously sustaining and destructive interrelationships of living creatures within the scope of their limited existences. While the poem's ironies preclude any presumption that its narrative voice can actually be heard by the bacteria and yeasts it addresses, Auden gestures toward what zoosemiotician Thomas Sebeok describes as the "rich arena of momentous semiotic events" that is the human skin itself, where "almost wholly out of awareness" we are "in intricate communicative interaction with the teeming faunal and floral inhabitants of that veritable microscopic dermal ecosystem."[36] A self-consciously shaped human verbal artifact, written in flat black codes on paper, functions for its reader at a great distance from the embodied voice of the poet, who himself can only speak *about* an intimate relationship he has with millions of other organisms that literally share his life. Yet the reader "hears" that voice in his or her mind and experiences a witty understanding of our close kinship with other creatures that includes intricate dialogues and responses within our very bodies, of bewildering complexities of interrelationship.

The value of an anti-Cartesian ecological sense of human experience portrayed in literary works such as these creates new habits of thought and engagement with the natural world, teaches a profound sense of kinship and interdependence among living things, and reinserts us conceptually in the ecological matrix we never have actually left. Merleau-Ponty's ecophenomenology offers a deeply nuanced theoretical description of reality that corresponds to the implications of modern life sciences and one that values literary openness to the mysteries of experience in the physical world. His account of the human place in nature accords with deep ecology's insistence on the common fate we share with other forms of life yet avoids the erasure of distinctions which Val Plumwood decries in deep ecology (163–165). Merleau-Ponty's thought seeks to avoid anthropocentrism, acknowledging the immanence of meaning in the world itself and therefore communicative modes outside human language, while at the same time describing the particular ways human art and literary forms allow the exploration of the invisible armature of the world we can see. Merleau-Ponty's description of human synergy with the rest of the living world parallels Jakob von Uexküll's description of the evolution of the octopus in call and response to its oceanic environment.

> The rule that governs the properties of sea-water acts upon the composition of the living chime of the cells of protoplasm of the octopus embryo. It shapes the melody of the development of the octopus form to express the properties of sea-water in a counterpoint; first and foremost, an organ is produced whose muscular walls force the water in and out. The rule of meaning

that joins point and counterpoint is expressed in the action of swimming.[37]

Although Merleau-Ponty subjected evolutionary biology to searching philosophical analysis, he assumed it to be the story of humankind's development. Human language, literature, and the other arts are for him the continuing efforts of our species to sing the world in call and response, carrying with them the past and anticipating the future.

CHAPTER

2

Animal Kin

W. H. Auden in his late poems offered a radical answer to the central question of humanism addressed by Pico della Mirandola, Montaigne, Hamlet, Descartes, Darwin, and Heidegger—what is the human? A marvelous chameleon, said Pico, who can move at will up and down the ladder of being and, at his best, leave the gross material body to become pure spirit, a pure contemplator even higher than the angels. Although disputed by Montaigne, this heroic notion of our species seemed culturally fixed in Descartes's formulation of the mechanical universe of *res extensa* distinguished from the *res cognitans* of human essence. In spite of Darwin's revolutionary theories that placed humans back within the community of animals, Western philosophy has vigorously resisted such a conclusion until very recently,[1] with no one more insistent than Heidegger on the abyss that separates us from other creatures. Why might it be that Auden and other poets and novelists were willing to embrace human kinship with nature when philosophers were not? As we saw in the previous chapter, Auden simply assumed his essential animality, rejoicing in his body's communal organization with millions of bacteria, yeasts, and tiny parasitic insects cozily interchanging nutrients and wastes together in their symbiotic dance of creation and destruction. This chapter asserts that if we acknowledge the history of life on the planet, we must accept Auden's sense of who we are, firmly based as it is in the biological discoveries of the past century,

45

as those continue to flesh out the story of our coevolution from previous life forms over millions of years. In other words, our common history with the rest of life must be central to any consideration of who we are and how we are related to our animal kin.

Lynn Margulis explains in *Symbiotic Planet* that each one of us is "a massive colony of microorganisms" (65). Her work in defining the early stages of evolution among the earliest bacteria represents some of the most important advances in evolutionary biology since the time of Auden's late poems. Contrary to the picture of the tiniest living organisms we inherited from Louis Pasteur's work on infection more than a hundred years ago, Margulis argues that it is more accurate to see the microbe as our colleague and ancestor (75).

> Recent work has revealed that the tiniest, most simple bacteria are very much like us. They continuously metabolize, using the same components as we do: proteins, fats, vitamins, nucleic acids, sugars, and other carbohydrates. It is true that even the simplest bacterium is extremely complex.... The more closely we study gene sequences and metabolism, the more we realize that all life since its origin has been similar to its brethren, all other life. (73)

Alphonso Lingis summarizes the consequences of research into the microbiology of the human body in terms which echo and move far beyond Auden's little poem.

> Human animals live in symbiosis with thousands of species of anaerobic bacteria, six hundred species in our mouths which neutralize the toxins all plants produce to ward off their enemies, four hundred species in our intestines, without which we could not digest and absorb the food we ingest. Some synthesize vitamins, others produce polysaccharides or sugars our bodies need. The number of microbes that colonize our bodies exceeds the number of cells in our bodies by up to a hundredfold. Macrophages in our bloodstream hunt and devour

trillions of bacteria and viruses entering our porous bodies continually. They replicate with their own DNA and RNA and not ours. ("Animal Body, Inhuman Face" 166)

This picture would make Heidegger cringe, because his adamant position on human uniqueness was based on a refusal to engage the findings of science.[2] While we have to acknowledge that the microbiotic work of Margulis and her colleagues was not available to Heidegger, neither was it available to Auden (or Virginia Woolf, Robinson Jeffers, John Steinbeck, or indeed Aldo Leopold or Rachel Carson). Yet Auden could already anticipate and appreciate the implications of such an understanding in biological discoveries of the 1960s. What was Heidegger afraid of, and why has philosophy yet to seriously engage the overwhelming evidence of human animality and kinship with the rest of the living community?[3]

To answer those questions, I suggest that we look far back in cultural history to a liminal time when our ancestors seemed to be divorcing themselves from immersion within the living world, attempting to shape a definition of humanity as some other kind of being. After a brief review of archaeological evidence for the emergence of distinctively human culture, we will examine a couple of ancient literary explorations of human-animal relationships. Then a brief reminder of formative positions in the European Renaissance will prepare for a return to consideration of Heidegger's, Derrida's, and Merleau-Ponty's philosophical positions on human relationships with other animals. Finally, an appeal to recent work in animal studies will demonstrate how many of the arguments about human exceptionalism have been eroded in the past few decades.

While contemporary biology has made it clear that each human individual is a microcosm of tiny symbionts and shares anatomical features and many basic behaviors with many other animals, we are at the same time quite distinct because of the particular species experience of the past five million years, when our primate family and chimpanzees split from a common ancestor. Physically and culturally, we developed from *Homo habilis* 2.5 million years ago, to

Homo erectus 1.7 million years ago, and then to *Homo sapiens* perhaps one hundred thousand years ago. Continuous adaptations and migrations were required for survival during the environmental changes of those enormous time spans, particularly the glacial advances and retreats from 500,000 BCE to the appearance of the first anatomically and culturally modern humans about fifty thousand years ago or perhaps even earlier.[4] These matters continue to be debated among archaeologists, anthropologists, linguists, and even genetic researchers as new evidence emerges and new theories are advanced. Indeed, it is hard to know exactly when to mark the first appearance of humans like us, as Merleau-Ponty made clear in his discussion of Teilhard de Chardin in the *Nature* lectures. As we saw in the previous chapter, he explained that we cannot see an exact moment for the appearance of humans with consciousness like our own, any more than we can see it in the ontogenesis of an individual human from an embryo (*N* 267).

Throughout this long period of emergence into our present state, we humans have been surrounded by and in various relations with all the other animals trying to survive. E. O. Wilson reminds us that

> for more than 99 percent of human history people have lived in hunter-gatherer bands totally and intimately involved with other organisms. During this period of deep history, and still farther back, into paleohominid times, they depended on an exact learned knowledge of crucial aspects of natural history. That much is true even of chimpanzees today, who use primitive tools and have a practical knowledge of plants and animals.[5]

Some animals such as lions and venomous snakes have been our enemies and predators; some such as fish and ruminants have been our prey; and some of the latter, such as oxen and horses, have been both prey and allies. Dogs and cats long ago formed alliances of convenience with humans, living cooperatively and coevolving.

While relationships with plants have also continuously developed during the long history of our kind, greater differences shape them and would be the subject of another line of exploration than mine. My present purpose is to establish the continual, dynamic, and inextricable interrelationship of humans and all the other animals throughout our existence, as the very ground on which the animal question must rest.[6]

Traditional peoples used to understand their interrelationships with other animals and their environment, though they would have described that understanding in rather different terms than ours.[7] Oral traditions from all over the world tell stories of humans conversing with other animals as relatives, being aided by them or tricked by them, and always remaining closely associated in a shared world, even though each may experience it in quite a different way. Acoma Pueblo Indian people of the American Southwest believe that their ancestors emerged from underground, aided by a wise spider and a locust.[8] People of my Pacific Northwest region tell stories of a woman who married a bear and turned into one (Erdoes and Ortiz 419–423), of another woman who made fun of frogs and was forced to marry one,[9] of trickster heroes Coyote or Raven who intervene in human and other creatures' affairs (Erdoes and Ortiz 171–172, 318–319, 344–346). Ancient Celts in Ireland believed that humans could turn into swans.[10] The development of agriculture and urban civilizations eroded that sense through a long, gradual process, but the earliest literatures are haunted by fears of what happens when humans try to set themselves outside or above these wider kinships. Let us now turn back to several of the earliest literary works documenting the uneasy sense of human-animal intertwining during the Bronze Age, when agriculture and cities were well established. These are the Mesopotamian *Epic of Gilgamesh* and "The Curse of Akkad," and Euripides's *Bakkhai*.

The Epic of Gilgamesh is the oldest known extended written narrative, a product of the complex agricultural civilization of Sumer, whose extensive walled cities and irrigation systems once dominated what is now the desertified landscape of Iraq. The power and appeal of Sumerian culture can be seen in the long life of the epic, which existed in Akkadian, Babylonian, and Hittite versions for fifteen hundred years before the cuneiform libraries of clay tablets were lost beneath the sands until nineteenth-century British archaeologists recovered them.[11] The fate of the rich world that produced the epic hints at the ecological problems encoded in it. And recently, of course, those problems have been rendered doubly poignant as what was left of Iraq's fertile landscapes has been devastated by years of modern warfare.

In *Pan's Travail*, J. Donald Hughes surveys the changed relationship between human beings and the environment in ancient Mesopotamia as the plow and systematic large-scale irrigation gave rise to the first great cities. The respectful, attentive attitudes of hunter-gatherers, early farmers, and herders toward the natural environment began to disappear. "It as if the barrier of city walls and the rectilinear pattern of canals had divided urban human beings from wild nature and substituted an attitude of confrontation for the earlier feeling of cooperation," he writes.[12] In *The Epic of Gilgamesh*, one can see this process symbolically enacted in a strange, dreamlike narrative of gigantic appetites, arrogant determination, and defiance of the sacred powers of the earth. The standard interpretations of the epic refer to deeds of courage and strength, battles with monsters, and themes such as "grief and the fear of death" or "love and vulnerability and the quest for wisdom."[13] But it is really a tale of ecological tragedy. Gilgamesh and his companion, Enkidu, arrogantly attack the powers of the natural world, figured as a huge cedar forest that is the dwelling place of the gods and location of the throne of Ishtar. The forest is guarded by the monster Humbaba, who personifies the energies of animal and plant life. Ishtar (Sumerian Inanna) herself is a great goddess of fertility and war and is also the Mistress of Animals. She was celebrated by an ancient cycle of Sumerian hymns and by the most sacred religious holiday of the Mesopotamian world. The Gilgamesh epic both begins and ends in paeans to her. It is very odd that the epic claims Gilgamesh's devotion to her and brags about his construction of her great temple, yet at the heart of the narrative, he contemptuously rejects and insults her. What this contradiction suggests is that Mesopotamian culture simultaneously revered her powers and gloried in the heroic king who dared to challenge her and to set human will above nature. The tragic consequences of that challenge provide the epic's dramatic and emotive force.

Central to the meaning of Gilgamesh and Enkidu's actions and fate are their complex symbolic relations with other animals. Before Enkidu enters Gilgamesh's life and accompanies him on the heroic journey to the cedar forest, we are told a troubling story about the young king, one that questions where wildness resides and how the boundaries from wild to tame, human to other animals, indeed male to female, can be blurred, crossed, policed, erased, restored. This introductory tale includes a kind of evolutionary movement from protohuman to civilized man, but in the end that supposed progression is profoundly questioned.[14]

As this introductory narrative opens the epic, we learn that young King Gilgamesh's behavior is so wild that it is devastating the city he is supposed to keep in order. Supposedly two-thirds god and one-third human, he is both "a mighty bank, protecting his warriors" and "a violent flood-wave, smashing a stone wall."

> In Uruk-the-Sheepfold he *walks* [*back and forth*],
>   like a wild bull lording it, head held aloft.
> He has no equal when his weapons are brandished.
>   (George 2–3)

The citizens of Uruk are oppressed by his outrageous energies and beg the gods for help, for "Gilgamesh lets no son go free to his father" and no girl go free to her mother or her bridegroom. How can this raging wild bull of a king be "the shepherd of Uruk-the-Sheepfold," guide and protector of his teeming people (George 4)?

In answer to the prayers of the people of Uruk and the complaints of the other gods, Anu orders the goddess Aruru, who created mankind, to create a counterpart or double for Gilgamesh. "Let him be a *match* for the storm of [Gilgamesh's] heart/let them vie with each other, so Uruk may be rested." Aruru washes her hands, pinches off some clay, and throws it into the wilderness.

> In the wild she created Enkidu, the hero,
>   offspring of Silence, knit strong by Ninurta.
>
> All his body is matted with hair,
>   he bears long tresses like those of a woman:
> the hair of his head grows thickly as barley,
>   he knows not a people, nor even a country.
>
> Coated in hair like the god of the animals,
>   with the gazelles he grazes on grasses,
> *joining the throng* with the game at the water-hole,
>   his heart *delighting* with the beasts in the water.
>   (George 5)

Enkidu is thus formed in a kind of Eden, as a primal human who seems to have both male and female qualities. He lives in harmony with the whole ecosystem of the grasslands around him. His food and drink are the same as that of the wild creatures, and he protects them from human trappers. Here, in contrast to the disruptive behavior of King Gilgamesh, wildness seems equated with cooperation, nurture, and balance.

Enkidu is domesticated by a priestess of the Temple of Inanna/Ishtar[15] at the request of a trapper who fears the hairy protohuman and resents his protection of the wild creatures. In an episode anticipating the biblical theft of Samson's energy by Delilah, the priestess Shamhat exposes her body to Enkidu so that he is aroused for six days and spends all his strength in lovemaking (George 8). The woman plays the classic mediating role between wildness and civilization which Donna Haraway has shown to be still operating in popular culture and in the discourse and semiotics of primatology with figures such as Jane Goodall and Dian Fossey.[16] With Enkidu's strength depleted, he is washed and shorn, given civilized clothing, and taught to eat and drink human nourishment. His wild animal companions now flee from him, and instead of being their protector, he becomes a guardian of shepherds. Then he travels to Uruk to meet his destined counterpart.

Gilgamesh is about to enter the House of Marriage when Enkidu finds him at last and blocks his entrance in rage. The exact meaning of Gilgamesh's role in the House of Marriage is unclear, as is Enkidu's behavior, but it can reasonably be interpreted as a reference to the ritual *hierogamy*, sacred in most Mesopotamian cultures, between the king and a representative of Inanna/Ishtar. This was the ceremony invoked in the Sumerian courtship hymns to Inanna and Dumuzi, and ordinary human procreation was understood to be similarly sacred, part of the cyclical flow of seasonal fertility among all animals and plants.[17] The *Epic of Gilgamesh* sets this sacred ritual in a negative context, with Enkidu moving violently to prevent Gilgamesh from enacting it. Like wild bulls, the two grapple together and shake the walls, smashing the doorposts. Once Gilgamesh triumphs, however, Enkidu vows allegiance to him, and they kiss each other and become inseparable companions, as the king's dreams foretold (George 15–17).

This bond replaces Gilgamesh's relationship with the fertile powers that Inanna/Ishtar represents, so that instead of acting in patterns that parallel the recurring cycles of life in the land, Gilgamesh sets himself against them. Gilgamesh's huge appetites focus on the ambition to make his name famous in the land forever, by attacking the great cedar forest.[18]

In this central episode of the narrative, a strange transference occurs between Enkidu and Gilgamesh, in which Enkidu tries to dissuade his friend from this plan, but then the roles reverse, with Enkidu urging him on once they have entered the forest. Enkidu has known the wild forest as one of its animal inhabitants, and he knows the power of Humbaba, whom the god Enlil has placed in the forest to guard it from intrusion. As they travel across the transitional spaces from city to wild landscape, and Enkidu uses his wilderness expertise to prepare their camping places, Gilgamesh has terrible dreams warning him about the dangers of trespassing here: mountains fall on him, a wild bull attacks him, and lightning strikes, turning his surroundings to cinders (George 30–35). The sacredness of the forest is clear even to these travelers once they enter its awesome precincts, but they only pause briefly before rushing on to attack Humbaba. The monster is in many ways a larger example of what Enkidu himself had been before he had known humankind; he has heroic qualities similar to the wild energies of both Gilgamesh and Enkidu. In the battle with Humbaba, Enkidu and Gilgamesh trade roles again, as Enkidu is at first terrified, but then Gilgamesh quails and Enkidu encourages him to attack, knowing that they must hasten before the gods learn what they are about and punish their sacrilege (George 43). This episode is saturated by a sense of forbidden behavior and certain retribution.

When Gilgamesh's axe severs Humbaba's neck, the forest trembles; he and Enkidu chop it down, pack up the great timbers, and float them down the Euphrates to Uruk. When they present the head of the monster to the gods, the ruling deity, Enlil, is enraged that his sacred wilderness and its guardian have been destroyed, and a council of gods decides that Enkidu must die in recompense (Sandars 80–84; George 55). Thus he and his monstrous wilderness double both perish as the sacred forest does; their lives were part of it, as Gilgamesh's is as well, by symbolic extension of his relationship with Enkidu. Gilgamesh lives on, but as a chastened man whose grief for Enkidu is so devastating that he is reduced to a figure very close to what Enkidu was before he traveled to Uruk. As Gilgamesh cries out in grief, he calls on the donkeys and gazelles to mourn him as Enkidu's parents and urges bears, hyenas, panthers, cheetahs, stags, jackals, lions, wild bulls, deer, and ibex—all the beasts of the wild—as well as the people of Uruk, to grieve for him (George 63–64). Gilgamesh strips himself of the emblems of his civilized power and all his clothing, reducing himself to the "poor, bare forked animal" of King Lear's unaccommodated man, with matted hair wandering in the wilderness, burned by sun and ice, hunting wild creatures and covered with their skins (George 71, 76–77). Though he wanders to the land of the dead in search of his friend, his impossible quest for eternal life ends in futility.

In the narrative's anguished examination of the shifting, uncertain boundaries between humans and other animals, *The Epic of Gilgamesh* demonstrates that their strengths and vitalities are shared and are part of the sacred energies of the landscape. But apparently human will cannot be controlled. Gilgamesh's arrogance leads him to commit terrible sacrilege, and the gods take their revenge on those who have devastated the natural world. Probably the inconsistencies and conflicting divine figures in the epic reflect conflicting cultural forces within ancient Sumerian and Babylonian and Assyrian societies, including some traditions that urge careful behavior within the natural environment that sustains all living things and some that support human exploitation of the landscape and its creatures. What is certain, however, is that the environment of ancient Mesopotamia changed disastrously as soils became salinated by intensive irrigation,[19] forests were cut down for the building of enormous cities, wild creatures were pushed out of their habitats by human activities, and the landscape was progressively impoverished. Somehow, in spite of the celebration of Gilgamesh and his marvelous city of Uruk, the epic understands the tragedy of human separation from the wider animal and plant community.

We now know that Mesopotamian civilizations suffered catastrophic destruction from climate change and environmental degradation by humans. In *Collapse*, Jared Diamond has examined a series of similar ecological disasters in other parts of the globe, caused by climate change in ancient times. Elizabeth Kolbert also describes the effects of climate change on many ancient societies but specifically focuses on the same world that produced *The Epic of Gilgamesh*. Clay tablets from the city of Akkad, just south of present-day Baghdad, preserve a lamentation called "The Curse of Akkad," describing the fall of a magnificent empire caused by impious behavior much like Gilgamesh's attack against the sacred cedar forest. Enlil, the god of winds and storms who punishes Enkidu in the Gilgamesh epic, is also the main deity in "The Curse of Akkad." He destroys King Naram-sin and all his people, who lived around 2200 BCE, some five hundred years after the historical King Gilgamesh. The lament describes how the fields produced no grain, the irrigated ponds no fish, and the irrigated orchards no syrup or wine. Clouds gathered, but no rain fell. "He who slept on the roof, died on the roof,/He who slept in the house, had no burial,/People were flailing at themselves from hunger."[20] Archaeological excavations at the site of ancient Akkad, together with soil samples taken from the site, show that about 2200 BCE a drought of terrible proportions coincided with the abandonment of human habitations and the death of the very soil. Even earthworms died out (Kolbert 66). This was also the time when the Old Kingdom of Egypt collapsed and villages in ancient Palestine were abandoned. It corresponds with a cold spell that drastically changed global climates, reducing rainfall in dry areas so severely that many forms of life simply disappeared for a time (Kolbert 72). The emerging historical record of human societies on the changing landscape of the planet begins to show that nature is far more dynamic and dangerous than nostalgic or escapist pastoral habits might lull us into thinking. *The Epic of Gilgamesh* and "The Curse of Akkad" express a grim Darwinian understanding that violent change and death are central to the natural world and that we humans must respect our fragile membership within it.[21]

Two thousand years after the life of the historical King Gilgamesh, Greek playwright Euripides wrote *The Bakkhai*, his version of an ancient tragedy that shares with the Gilgamesh epic many anxieties about human-animal relationships and the tragic consequences of pretending that they do not exist.[22] The story of King Pentheus's demise also involves an arrogant young king who tries to impose human will on nature, an epicene doppelganger who is closely associated with wild animals, shifting boundaries between human and nonhuman forms, and death as the consequence for defying the sacred powers of the natural world.

Friedrich Nietzsche, at least in part under the influence of Darwinian thought,[23] identified Dionysos with natural forces and implied that Pentheus's efforts to resist his divine cousin and enforce his will on these energies exemplified an Apollonian extreme.[24] But *The Birth of Tragedy* looks rather quaint in its rhapsodic appeal to an opposition that is not an explicit part of Euripides's text, a text in which Apollo is only mentioned once. Instead a close examination of the tragedy reveals that both Pentheus and Dionysos are intimately animal, both having strange genealogies including snaky, bovine, and leonine forbears, both metamorphosing into some of these different species at given points in the play. Boundaries and distinctions among species are not at all secure in this strange world. The tragedy that reenacts the sacrifice by which Dionysos is torn to pieces in some versions of his myths comes about because Pentheus refuses to acknowledge his own animality and the wild forces embodied in and manipulated by his divine double. Translator Robert Bagg describes "Euripides's bitter vision of an implacable divine presence not outside, but *within* our nature, a presence utterly hostile to what we uneasily call our humanity."[25] One could qualify Bagg's point, however, by suggesting that the only reason this divine presence becomes so implacable and violent in the events we witness is that Pentheus enrages the god by refusing to worship him.

Pentheus and Dionysos (or Bakkhus) are about the same age and look similar, except that Dionysos has flowing hair and almost feminine features, while Pentheus is a hypermasculine military man determined to condemn the god's worship in his city of Thebes. The Chorus of Maenad worshipers informs the audience that Dionysos was born bull-headed and writhing with snakes in Crete. He is also associated with twining ivy, leopards and lions, and of course with the grape (Dodds 76–79). But Pentheus himself is the son of a man whose name, Echion, means "snake" and who sprang up from the earth when Kadmos, the slayer of a mighty serpent, sowed the monster's teeth in the earth (Bagg 8, 28). The Chorus informs the audience,

> There is evil in Pentheus's blood—
> the bestial earth blazes in his face,
> an inhuman snake face
> like those his giant fathers had,
> those butchers who were beaten
> when they tried to fight gods.
> (Bagg 37)

Kadmos is Pentheus's grandfather, whose daughter Agave married this serpent's offspring, and Dionysos announces at the end of the play that he will turn Kadmos and his daughter into serpents to punish them for their impiety (Bagg 66–67).[26]

This genealogy remains just under the surface of the play's action but is hinted at frequently by puns and choral epithets for the god, as both E. R. Dodds and Robert Bagg point out in their introductions to the text, and the Greek audience would have been fully attuned to these uncanny associations. But Pentheus is so determined to maintain his rational, human control of himself and his kingdom that he has buried them far from his consciousness. When he confronts the young stranger who is Dionysos in disguise, he is alternately attracted and infuriated by him. He tries to chain him up and throw him in prison, but the stranger turns into a wild bull and cannot be held by his jailers. Pentheus's sacrilege is punished by earthquake and fire, yet the young king refuses to understand (Bagg 40–41). Finally, Dionysos so befuddles him that he agrees to dress in women's clothes and go to spy on the Bakkhic worship performed by his mother and the other women, outside the city in the pastoral space of wild meadows and hills. By this point, Pentheus's vision is blurred, so that when he looks at the magical stranger, he sees him trotting like a bull, with horns sprouting from his head. Pentheus wonders whether he is seeing distortions and asks Dionysos, "were you always . . . animal? / There's no question you're a bull now" (Bagg 50).

Animal Kin

The fatal climax happens offstage, when the worshipers see Pentheus spying from his hiding place in a tree, tear it down, and rip him to pieces in the ritual practices of *sparagmos* and *omophagia* central to ancient Dionysian worship—the tearing to pieces of a live animal and the eating of its raw flesh (Dodds xvi–xix; Bagg 56–57). The women think they have captured a lion, and Pentheus's mother, Agave, proudly displays his head as they come in triumph back to Thebes. "I took this yearling lion / without ropes. Look at him!!" she cries to the Chorus (Bagg 58). Although this instance of the god's worship is particularly gruesome, it implies a general truth, that there is no resisting the metamorphosis of animal forms, of which humans are only a temporary manifestation. Eating and drinking, the nourishing of human bodies, requires violent tearing of other bodies and ingesting their flesh. Because Pentheus and his mother refused to acknowledge their subordinate part in this sacrificial economy and their dependence on the powers of the natural world which Dionysos represents, they become sacrificial victims themselves. The Chorus has forewarned of such retribution for human arrogance in the face of nature's power.

> The gods work slowly,
> but you can trust them—
> their power breaks all
> mad arrogant men
> who love foolishness
> and pay no mind to the gods—
> but the gods are devious
> and in no hurry—
> they put
> an impious man at his ease, then
> hunt him down.
> ....
> It costs little to believe,
> that, whatever divinity is,
> it is power;

> which time seasons, strengthens
> and lets stand—
> such laws are Nature herself
> coming to flower.
>
> (Bagg 48–49)

The moral structures of Euripides's play are complex and confusing, but at its heart is the insistence on human kinship with all other life in both harmonious and violent relationships which cannot long be denied or resisted.

Both *The Epic of Gilgamesh* and *The Bakkhai* are very ancient literary works, liminal in their attempts to rationalize traditional beliefs about human relationships with other animals and the wild energies Merleau-Ponty associated with the Brute being that permeates all life, while also retaining deep fears about the costs of civilization with its presumptions of separation from nature and all other animals. Examples of other such ancient works can be multiplied from many cultures, but those I have chosen to discuss are demonstrable predecessors of our own European/Mediterranean background. In the millennia that have intervened since they were written, anxieties about human membership in the larger biotic community seem gradually to have ebbed, as the apparent control of the nonhuman world and other animals by our species increased. Since the Industrial Revolution of the eighteenth and nineteenth centuries, developing technologies have seemed to prove the superiority of *Homo sapiens* over all others.

As Arthur Lovejoy established long ago, the patterns of dualistic thought in European culture which separate humans from nature and other animals, mind from body, and spirit from matter can be traced back in strong, explicit written form at least as far as Plato.[27] But such views remained a sort of otherworldly "official philosophy" which did not fully engage the popular mind. That is because "most men, however much they may have professed to accept it, . . . have never quite believed it, since they have never been able to deny to the things disclosed by the senses a genuine and imposing and highly important kind of realness." Indeed, most people have "manifestly continued to find something very solid and engrossing in the world in which [their] own constitution was so deeply rooted and with which it was so intimately interwoven" (26–27). Thus, in spite of the dualism inherent in Christianity, many older forms of animism were absorbed into northern European practices of the faith, most notably in Celtic reverence for sacred springs and groves and relationships with animals in poetry, saints' lives, and popular legends found in Ireland, Cornwall, Wales, and Brittany (Jackson, *A Celtic Miscellany* 277–305). Medieval bestiaries also continued long habits of associations between people and the living communities around them, though framed in allegorical Christian terms.

With Renaissance humanism, Enlightenment optimism, and the triumph of scientific thought, however, such attitudes went into eclipse for several hundred years. In spite of extreme exaltations of human capacities, such as Pico della Mirandola's, however, skeptics such as Michel de Montaigne and William Shakespeare disputed this kind of complacency. Montaigne's "Apology for Raymond Sebond" is primarily a sustained attack on the notion that humans are superior to other animals.

> The most vulnerable and frail of all creatures is man, and at the same time the most arrogant. . . . [By the vanity of his imagination] he equals himself to God, attributes to himself divine characteristics, picks himself out and separates himself from the horde of other creatures, carves out their shares to his fellows and companions the animals, and distributes among them such portions of faculties and powers as he sees fit.[28]

As Darwin was to do four hundred years later, Montaigne asserted that animals reason and feel emotions, communicate with those of their own species and also with those of different species, and make their way through the world as active and capable agents just as humans do (331–358). In pastoral comedies such as *A Midsummer*

Night's Dream and *As You Like It*, Shakespeare satirized the conventional poses of courtly folk pretending to be shepherds, using forest settings to expose human folly and weakness in contrast to natural forces and to suggest closer relationships to other animals than humanist assumptions presumed. In *Hamlet*, Shakespeare began to show clear Montaignian influences, and scholars have long associated Hamlet's anguished probing of human nature in the famous soliloquies with Montaigne's *Essays*.[29] But the antipastoral *King Lear* brings us closest to Montaigne's picture of humanity in "The Apology for Raymond Sebond." When the old king has defied his cruel daughters and run out of the shelter of the human community into the storm on the heath, he abandons his arrogance and at last comes to see himself as an "unaccommodated man" like Tom O'Bedlam, "a poor, bare, fork'd animal."[30]

Such skepticism was pushed to the edges of European thought by the determined quest for certainty of Newton and Descartes in the early decades of the seventeenth century, as we saw in the previous chapter. Perhaps as part of a reaction against Enlightenment reason, or the blight of industrial cities, certainly in part as a product of imperialism, which sent Europeans off on exotic natural history quests all over the globe, in the nineteenth century a renewed fascination with the animal world and the planet's history gave birth to a wave of life sciences, with Darwin's work as a climactic breakthrough that initiated a radical rethinking of the human place in the world.

Not only did Darwin assemble a powerful body of biological evidence for the evolution of life forms, from the work of many contemporaries as well as his own careful studies in *The Origin of Species*, but in *The Descent of Man* he also insisted on attention to "the weighty arguments derived from the nature of the affinities which connect together whole groups of organisms," specifically "the homological structure, embryological development, and rudimentary organs" that favor evolutionary kinship.[31] Already by 1871, scientists from all over Europe, such as Thomas Henry Huxley, Th. L. W. Bischoff, and Edme Vulpian, had demonstrated the similarity in skeletal structures and brain formation and function of humans and other primates, as well as the common vulnerability of many animals to the same diseases humans suffer, such as "hydrophobia, variola, the glanders, syphilis, cholera, herpes, &c.," which proves close similarity of tissues and blood (Darwin 11). The same medicines are efficacious across these species. Reproductive processes are strikingly similar, and embryological development is almost indistinguishable until the later stages of development. Human embryos look much like those of dogs in the early weeks, and all mammals begin their embryonic forms with gills and tails (10–17). Darwin goes on to assert that animals share most of the subjective feelings and cognitive abilities of humans. They manifest the same kinds of emotions, they have similar imaginative lives, they reason, and they build structures which shape their material surroundings to their needs (34–53).[32]

In spite of Darwin's enormous influence from the late nineteenth century through the twentieth, modern urban life and its increasing technological sophistication have allowed popular culture and much of intellectual life to continue operating from Enlightenment assumptions about human superiority to all other life and essential separation from it. In recent decades, however, pressure for change has been growing. As we have seen, recent work in evolutionary biology by scientists such as Lynn Margulis shows why the evolution of life forms makes it untenable to think of our kind as the summit of creation. "We need to be freed from our species specific arrogance," she writes. "No evidence exists that we are 'chosen,' the unique species for which all the others are made" (119). Frans de Waal agrees, having concluded from a career of studying the culture of chimpanzees and other primates,

> The time has come to define the human species against the backdrop of the vast common ground we share with other life forms. Instead of being tied to how we are unlike any animal, human identity should be built around how we are animals that have taken certain capacities a significant step farther.

We and other animals are both similar and different, and the former is the only sensible framework within which to flesh out the latter. (*Ape* 362)

De Waal's view is shared by more and more ethologists, primatologists, and animal researchers. The popularity of nature documentaries since the 1950s has drawn the general public as well to think increasingly of other animals as sympathetic creatures on their own terms. Mary Midgley speaks of the popular imagination as being struck rather suddenly by a flood of new information about animals. "Some dim conception of splendours and miseries hitherto undreamt of, of the vast range of sentient life, of the richness and complexity found in even the simplest creatures, has started to penetrate even to the least imaginative."[33]

Even so, academic disciplines, public policy, technology, and agriculture remain entangled in humanist traditions of exceptionalism which continue to motivate the treatment of animals all over the globe. Jacques Derrida believed that during the past two hundred years we have "been involved in an unprecedented transformation" of our relationship with other animals, resulting in their subjection by science and technology of *"unprecedented* proportions," particularly in industrial agriculture (*Animal* 24–25). To interpret this crisis, he interrogates Western philosophical tradition from Aristotle to Heidegger, from Descartes to Kant, Levinas, and Lacan (27), but the center of his focus is Heidegger, the most powerful modern advocate for the humanist exaltation of our species in determined rejection of essential kinship among animals within a shared evolutionary history.[34] As a context for Derrida's particular criticisms, we need to revisit Heidegger's main arguments. Then we can look more closely into Derrida's efforts to deconstruct traditions of human exceptionalism and more recent developments in that conversation about "the animal question," on the way to examining Merleau-Ponty's efforts to reconsider such ideas from the perspective of evolutionary biology and animal studies in the *Nature* lectures. Finally, a sampling of recent ethological and primatological studies will demonstrate how careful attention to actual animals has undermined the possibility of maintaining a firm separation of our species from the animal others that surround us. That is a crucial direction which Derrida criticizes other philosophers for not taking, though he does not follow it himself (*Animal* 89).

Soon after *Being and Time*, Heidegger gave a lecture course called *The Fundamental Concepts of Metaphysics* (1929–1930), which his translators, William McNeill and Nicholas Walker, describe as making an astonishing move into biology. As they explain, nowhere else in his career did he "take the experimental results of science so seriously in support of possible metaphysical claims."[35] But what is peculiar here is the resolutely negative way in which he interpreted what he found. After a rather simplistic discussion of bees as representative examples of instinctive "drivenness" among animals, Heidegger focused particularly on the work of Hans Driesch on entelechy and on Jakob von Uexküll's careful demonstrations of the subjectivity and agency of various animals. But rather than considering the possibilities of the organism's unfolding development in ways not predictable from its earliest form, or recognizing the world-forming implications of Uexküll's *Umwelten* theory, Heidegger rejected Driesch's entelechy findings as "vitalism" and saw Uexküll's *Umwelt* as an encircling ring that limits the animal's behavior (see Agamben 51–52). This "disinhibiting ring is . . . something with which the animal encircles itself as long as it lives," struggling to fulfill its instinctual drives (Heidegger, *Fundamental* 259–264). Thus animals are essentially captivated.

The overarching premise leading Heidegger to such conclusions is his argument that animals are "poor in world." This position is based on unexamined claims about the special place of humans in the world that echo the biblical story of Genesis 1, in which God gives mastery of all the earth's creatures to the human species created in the divine image.[36] Heidegger flatly states that "man is not simply regarded as a part of the world" but stands over against it, in "a '*having*' of world as that in which man moves, and with which he engages. Thus man is, first, a part of the world, and second, as this part he is at once both master and servant of the world" (*Fundamental* 176–177). In this position, he is "world-forming" because he alone of creatures can know things "as such" and can let them be to manifest themselves (177, 264, 270, 275). Man forms world because of the *Dasein* in him (literally "being there," or where Being comes into presence), which brings world forth. He sets it forth by giving an image or view of the world and thus constitutes the world, containing and embracing it (285).

This position asserting human mastery precedes any discussion of particular animals and justifies Heidegger's accompanying assertion that animals are "poor in world." The accessibility of beings which *Dasein* allows humans is not available to "the animal" (*Fundamental* 199). *Dasein* allows humans to transpose themselves into animals, that is, to understand their spheres of living to some degree, "being able to go along with the other being while remaining *other* with respect to it" (203, 210–211). The reverse, in Heidegger's view, is not possible; animals cannot transpose themselves into humans or share *Dasein*. They cannot contemplate things "as such" but remain captivated within the limiting sphere of their driven, instinctual life. Using the example of domestic animals such as dogs and cats, Heidegger simply states that they serve the house in which they live; "they *'live' with us*. But we do not live with them if living means: *being* in an animal kind of way." And our being with them does not mean "*existing-with*, because a dog does not exist but merely lives." Dogs and cats may feed with us, but they do not eat as we do (210). Heidegger claims that "this talk of poverty in world and world-formation must not be taken as a hierarchical evaluation" (194), and yet it is hard to see how else to take it. The essence of animality which Heidegger seeks to define in these passages is radical limitation, poverty in world, and with domestic animals, a subservient position within human-controlled realms. One wonders how he could know this. Humans might look similarly limited or captivated from an outside point of view, that of a crow for instance, seeing that humans cannot fly up into a tree after it. Or from the perspective of a domestic cat or dog, a human could seem severely deprived in sensory intelligence such as the ability to smell the recent passage of other creatures on a path, to hear the approach of a familiar engine several blocks away, or to see in the dark. Similarly a cat could observe that a human could not quickly run up a tree to flee a predator. But Heidegger does not consider such possibilities.

Much later, after World War II, Heidegger wrote his "Letter on Humanism" to a young Frenchman who questioned him about Sartre's emphasis on subjectivity as the basis of humanism. Heidegger rejected this as a reliance on the Cartesian *cogito* and sought instead to focus on man's unique position in the lighting of being.[37] In spite of the philosophical subtleties and technicalities of his arguments, he seems unable to escape the traditional humanist dualism of mind and body, going so far as to claim that "the human body is something essentially other than an animal organism" ("Letter" 204).[38] Yet here he confronts what de Waal calls the "embarrassing problem" that continues to bedevil philosophers (*Ape* 41). Heidegger names it as "our appalling and scarcely conceivable bodily kinship with the beast" ("Letter" 206). To preserve human uniqueness and superiority from the horrors of this kinship, Heidegger insists on the famous abyss yawning between ourselves and living creatures most closely related to us. It is defined by language, which he says we have and other animals do not. Thus he retreats into the essentially humanist idealism of Plato, Pico, and Descartes, mystifying language as something which is not "the utterance of an organism" but instead "the lighting-concealing advent of Being itself." This is the "ek-static character of Dasein" by which man takes the lighting of Being into his care (206–207).

Finally, in Heidegger's 1951–1952 lectures (*Was heisst denken?*; English translation, *What Is Called Thinking?*), he makes his most surprising claim—that apes do not have hands. Here he challenges Darwin's assertions about bodily similarities among mammals with the most extreme possible example—chimpanzees, orangutans, and gorillas—the primates whose limbs, features, and even many behaviors are so much like ours. To refute the morphology argument which he had been rejecting as early as the 1929–1930 lectures,

Heidegger relies once more on subjective states and behaviors linked to *Dasein* and human ethics. Other animals have mere grasping organs such as paws, claws, or fangs, but "only a being who can speak, that is, think, can have hands." Human hands not only grasp or catch but reach, receive, extend welcome, hold, design, and sign. This is the meaning of handicraft. "Every motion of the hand in every one of its works carries itself through the element of thinking, every bearing of the hand bears itself in that element. All the work of the hand is rooted in thinking."[39]

In 1983, Jacques Derrida deplored this argument as dogmatically humanist, a willful refusal to take account of the accumulating and increasingly refined zoological knowledge of apes and other animals ("Heidegger's Hand" 173–175). The final decades of Derrida's life were devoted to extensive considerations of "the animal question" and an attempt to systematically dismantle the dominant human-exceptionalist position of philosophical tradition in the West. (See for example the essays listed in the bibliography.) The fullest expression of his conclusions came in the Cerisy lectures of 1997 and their posthumous publication as *The Animal That Therefore I Am*, which Cary Wolfe calls "arguably the single most important event in the brief history of animal studies."[40] This work begins (in spite of Derrida's disclaimer) with a primal scene that playfully reimagines Montaigne's 1592 musing in "The Apology for Raymond Sebond" about whether "when I play with my cat [*ma chatte*], who knows if I am not a pastime to her more than she is to me?" (*Animal* 6–11). Derrida makes the situation more dramatic with a Freudian twist, by concentrating on his own sense of shame when his cat gazes at his naked body in a frontal exposure that allows his sex to be the focus of attention (4–7). He insists that this is his actual cat, a female, rather than some allegorical figure, but as Donna Haraway notes, he does not really consider "what the cat might actually be doing, feeling, thinking," and we hear no more about her for the rest of this long lecture (*When Species Meet* 20). Seemingly comic or ridiculous, the situation allows Derrida to strip the human animal to its naked self and to think about all the coverings we have shaped and fitted to protect us from the weather and from a recognition of who we are. Other animals have no need to do this and no shame at being simply their bodily selves. "Dressing oneself would be inseparable from all the other figures of what is 'proper to man,' even if one talks about it less than speech or reason, the *logos*, history, laughing, mourning, burial, the gift, etc." (Derrida, *Animal* 5).

The second section of the ten-hour Cerisy seminar[41] begins with Derrida's parodic echo of Montaigne's famous question "Que sçay-je?" (*Complete Essays* 508) or "What do I know?" that follows Descartes to ask instead, "Mais moi, que suis-je?"—"But I, who am I?" This question simultaneously puns on the verb *suivre*, whose first-person indicative form is also *suis*, to ask, "Who am I following?" (*L'animal que donc je suis* 113; trans. in *Animal* as "But as for me, who am I (following)?" [52]). The whole question of the human becomes at once the question of animality, with the witty implication of evolutionary links to other animals hovering around its exploration. Oddly enough, however, Derrida does not take up this evolutionary suggestion, even though he does speak briefly of succession or inheritance. Perhaps it was only an unconscious possibility that was shadowing *him*, since as we shall see later, he insistently refuses to consider any biological continuity between humans and other animals. Instead, by "following," he wants to play with the implications of chasing, hunting, training, and taming animals. He also means to consider the differing spatial modes of "Being *after*, being *alongside*, being *near* [près]" or *being-with* animals. He seeks to examine the pressures of these modes of relationship with this absolute other, his gaze on the animal or its view of him and a sense of being surrounded by "the animal" (*Animal* 10–11).

Repeatedly Derrida comments on the fact that most philosophers who have pontificated about the differences between humans and other animals have never considered the animals' gaze on them. "They neither wanted nor had the capacity to draw any systematic consequence from the fact that an animal could, facing them, look at them, clothed or naked, and in a word, without a word, *address them* . . . from down there, from a wholly other origin" (13–14).

In particular, he names Descartes, Kant, Heidegger, Levinas, and Lacan, who never evoke the possibility of the animal's sentient consideration of us as beings (89–90). They fail to distinguish animals from one another but instead collapse them into one category that stands on the other side of an abyss from humans, who are "subjects or *Daseins* of an 'I think,' 'I am,' along the line of a single common trait and on the other side of a single, indivisible limit" (90). Derrida goes back to Genesis to follow or ferret out the track of a whole history of human disavowal of relationship and reciprocity with other animals to the present. His untangling of this tradition is witty, searching, and rich, but it is too complex to explore adequately here. Seeking to "break with the Cartesian tradition of the animal-machine without language and without response" (119), he engages the classic ethical issue of animals' potential to suffer and the industrial massacre of animals that has turned traditional relations between species upside down and can be compared to the worst cases of genocide (24–29). He insists that we distinguish among animal species and individuals rather than lumping all of them into a generic concept (41, 47–48), and he considers whether animals respond to humans (119–140). But what seems to me central in his examination of cultural and philosophical tradition is his confrontation with Heidegger's claim that animals are poor in world and have no access to *Dasein*. Turning Heidegger's assertion on its head, Derrida asks, "Can one, even in the name of fiction, think of a world without animals, or at the very least a world poor in animals, . . . Is being-with-the-animal a fundamental and irreducible structure of being-in-the-world . . . ?" (79). And he identifies moments when Heidegger himself admits that "we don't finally know what world is! At bottom it is a very obscure concept!" (151).

Turning away from Heidegger at last, Derrida urges a profound consideration of what *being with* animals really means. He opens the door to exploring the work of primatologists (89, 90, 99), and he implies various kinds of animal sentience in calling for a pluralization of the "as such," so that we consider the possibility of other animals' thinking about things *as things* in various ways not necessarily like human ways. Indeed, he finally wonders whether even human beings have the "as such" (160).

In spite of these moves toward acknowledging fuller lives for animals, Derrida continues Heidegger's emphasis on an abyssal divide between them and ourselves, refusing to accept the much deeper evolutionary kinship that more than a century of scientific evidence supports. Matthew Calarco wonders why Derrida would resolutely refuse to abandon the human-animal distinction and "why he would use this language of ruptures and abysses when the largest bodies of empirical knowledge we have concerning human beings and animals strongly contest such language" (145, 147). But Derrida explicitly resists any claims of "biological continuism, whose sinister connotations we are well aware of" (*Animal* 30–31). It is easy to understand why as a Jew he might have been particularly aware of the cruel history of Social Darwinism, eugenics, and animal coding for abjecting human groups during the twentieth century. However, accepting a continuum between our species and other creatures need not lead to extremes such as Social Darwinism or some of the excesses of sociobiology and Neo-Darwinism which include humans within mechanistic and reductionist descriptions of organic behavior. A continuum would instead imply that many kinds of consciousness and perception evolved over the hundreds of millennia of life's emergence. Human sentience would then be understood as one of many kinds of animal awareness, as the work of Uexküll shows. Neither humans nor other animals could then be dismissed deterministically as mechanisms; instead they would have to be recognized as active participants in shaping the many meanings of the biological community.

Failure to admit the ancient and continuing kinship of humans with other animals, and our accompanying place deep within the community of living creatures, ignores the indisputable fact that we are literally made from the same stuff as the rest of it. Such an assertion does not push kinship so far that humans arrogantly engulf all the natural world within ourselves, as Val Plumwood charged about the impulses of deep ecology (166–167), or that humanity and nature collapse into "a predictable, continuous, and homogenous unity," as Ted Toadvine suggested more recently ("Primacy of Desire" 140). Calarco believes that Derrida's fear of continuism derives from a false dilemma of that kind (148–149). To say that everything is composed of atoms and molecules is to assert material continuism, but no one would then claim that all beings and objects and forces are therefore indistinguishable. Similarly, human kinship with other animals is not identity (Midgley, *Ethical Primate* 131); we may share more than 98 percent of our genetic makeup with chimpanzees, but we are clearly different in stature, strength, body hair, ability to swing from tree to tree, and of course cultures and methods of communication. In fact, the developing evolutionary continuum of life forms on earth emphatically answers Derrida's question of whether "being-with-the-animal [is] a fundamental and irreducible structure of being-in-the-world." Our very bodies attest to the impossibility of a world without animals and to our own biological enmeshment within and inclusion on a continuum of other creatures.

Derrida's final work set off a flurry of related debates on the question of the animal, but most of the discussion has until recently remained trapped within Heidegger's formulation of the abyssal separation of humans from other animals, without serious attention to the implications of work in animal sciences of the past half century. In *The Open*, for example, Giorgio Agamben critiques the idea of the traditional conceptual processes which he calls the "anthropological machine" that produces the concept of the human by separating it from the animal realm, but he nevertheless continues to assume a necessary, defining separation (16; see also 92).

From a different angle, Kelly Oliver seeks to counter both Heidegger and Agamben with Merleau-Ponty's notion of "strange kinship" between humans and other animals, but she continues Derrida's refusal to consider evolutionary continuism.[42] Although Oliver sees many of the same differences between Heidegger's and Merleau-Ponty's approaches to animality that I have stressed, she sees Merleau-Ponty as anthropocentric in a way that I do not, and she denies that the continuity he describes between humans and other animals is an evolutionary relationship. She claims that, like Heidegger, he develops a concept of animality and examines scientific studies of particular animals only "to reinforce his notions about the role of perception and behavior in man." And she charges that, like Heidegger, "Merleau-Ponty pokes and probes laboratory animals in the name of science," thinking of them as objects, rather than considering everyday experiences with animals.[43] In the next chapter, I make the case that, on the contrary, Merleau-Ponty's attention to animals in his late work is primarily at the service of his overall ontology of intertwining creatures in an environment of Wild or Brute Being and that he saw the evolution of life forms as the basis for understanding the place and character of our own species within the dynamic flesh of the world.

Notable exceptions to the tendency of insisting on human separation from other animals in recent debates have been the positions of Donna Haraway, Cary Wolfe, and Glen Mazis. Haraway's *When Species Meet* continues her radical critique of human exceptionalism and species boundaries that was begun twenty years ago in *Primate Visions* and further developed in *Simians, Cyborgs, and Women* and her work on genetic engineering in *Modest Witness*. Haraway sees humans entangled among knots of interspecies relationships and symbioses, as dancers in "constitutive intra-action at every folded layer of time and space. These are the contagions and infections that wound the primary narcissism of those who still dream of human exceptionalism" (*When Species Meet* 32). In *Zoographies*, Matthew Calarco approaches the issue as a philosopher, carefully reviewing the animal question from Heidegger to Derrida and agreeing with Haraway's view, suggesting that "*we could simply let the human-animal distinction go*" (149).

Cary Wolfe's groundbreaking *Animal Rites* (2003) and the collection of essays he edited on the animal question, *Zoontologies* (2003) initiated a surge of new work on the subject. "In the Shadow of Wittgenstein's Lion," chapter 2 of *Animal Rites* and also included in *Zoontologies*, is a theoretically rigorous survey of the arguments within critical theory, pivoting around and carefully analyzing

Derrida's position. More recently, Wolfe has come to an explicit position that urges a return to considering "the thickness and finitude of human embodiment and to human evolution as itself a specific form of animality, one that is unique and different from other forms but no more different, perhaps, than an orangutan is from a starfish" ("Human" 572). This appears in the March 2009 special *PMLA* focus on animal studies highlighting a variety of efforts now under way to define posthuman, or at least posthumanist, accounts of who we are and where our cultural activities fit in an ecological understanding of the world. In the same issue, Ursula Heise suggests that we assume a continuum from android through animal modes of being, of the kind explored in contemporary science fiction.[44] Other articles, by Susan McHugh, Kimberly Benston, Bruce Boehrer, and Una Chaudhuri, consider animal agents in literature, animal studies and the deconstruction of character, the animal bases of human performance, and the relation of critical animal studies to scientific experimentation on animals.[45] Timothy Morton attempts in "Ecologocentrism: Unworking Animals" to use the Derridean concept of *différance* to claim that ecological thinking does not allow us to posit a distance between ourselves and the rest of the world.[46] All this work explores how animal studies have troubled or dissolved previously assumed species barriers and now are shaping new ethical and cultural presumptions.

Strangely, Merleau-Ponty is almost never mentioned in these writings, even though he was already moving beyond human exceptionalism in the 1950s and seriously engaged in questioning the philosophical consequences of biological and ethological research. Why are the recent debates around the subject ignoring his work? Taylor Carman and Mark Hansen believe one reason is that Merleau-Ponty's premature death prevented the full development of his philosophical project. They also suggest that his reputation fell victim to the radical spirit of 1968, which led a younger generation including Derrida, Lacan, and Foucault to lump Merleau-Ponty together with Husserl and Sartre and to accuse phenomenology of humanist focus on consciousness, or subjectivism.[47]

In fact, that charge could not have been made if Merleau-Ponty's late writings and lectures had been well known, as Glen Mazis has recently made clear in his illuminating exploration of Merleau-Ponty's late work in *Humans, Animals, Machines: Blurring Boundaries*. Not only did Merleau-Ponty reject that kind of focus on human consciousness, but he went well beyond the positions of other phenomenologists by describing humans as completely intertwined with the dynamic matrix of what Husserl called the lifeworld. Renaud Barbaras explains that Merleau-Ponty's main purpose throughout his career was to complete Husserl's project by closely examining our participation within the whole of that living community. Barbaras sees the strength and originality of his approach in "its taking into account the specificity of life, of the biological life, as the *identity of reality* and phenomenon."[48] As we have seen, *The Visible and the Invisible* offers a philosophy of life that is intrinsically ecological and accords with evolution in a way that moves far beyond any other philosopher, except perhaps the American pragmatist John Dewey.[49] Unlike all the philosophers Derrida criticizes for never considering the vast body of research on actual animals, the *Nature* lectures reveal the kind of exploratory engagement with animal studies that Derrida urged on philosophers half a century later.

However, Merleau-Ponty's position on human-animal relations in his late work is deeply complicated by its unfinished quality. As we have seen in the previous chapter, the manuscript of what came to be posthumously published as *The Visible and the Invisible* was relatively polished and carefully worked out as far as it went, but only the first section of his three-part project was completed.[50] At the same time that he was working on the first section, he was testing out the second part of the project, Nature, in his lectures at the Collège de France from 1956 to 1960. These lectures are centrally important for my purposes, because they show his careful way of engaging the scientific discoveries of his own time, particularly in biology and animal studies, which are so necessary for ecological understanding and environmental philosophy. But as translator

Robert Vallier explains, we have no precise record of their content, and the lectures themselves were explorations, quite freely improvised from sparse notes that sometimes consisted only of bibliographies with a few citations or scribbled ideas.[51] The anonymous student whose notes are the primary record of those lectures was careful and attentive but could not have captured every word accurately. "This situation makes it difficult for the interpreter to say with certitude that 'Merleau-Ponty thought this' or 'argued that'" (Vallier xiv). Because there were no student notes for the third course, "Nature and Logos: The Human Body," Merleau-Ponty's own fragmentary notes for the lectures have been translated, though they are difficult to decipher as well as to fully understand. Even so, as Vallier says, the notes do allow us "to see Merleau-Ponty's thinking in action, unfolding itself, groping its way to expression, coming into its own" (xv), and we can extrapolate his suggestions and questions to resonate with more recent biological discoveries and debates about human-animal relations.

The Visible and the Invisible is unequivocal in asserting the essential wildness of Being and the intertwining, or chiasmic relationships, among all creatures and things in the dynamic unfolding of reality through evolutionary time. Human beings, like all other living things, are immersed in this *flesh* of the world, within "a spatial and temporal pulp where the individuals are formed by differentiation" (*VI* 114). Within this flesh, species and individual organisms manifest not only formal resemblances but also identical constituting substances, that is, microorganisms that embody or mirror biological macrocosms. Heidegger would be horrified to think that each human or other animal body was itself a symbiotic community of many tinier bodies. Yet this new understanding would not have troubled Merleau-Ponty, who asked, "Why would not the synergy exist among different organisms, if it is possible within each? Their landscapes interweave, their actions and their passions fit together exactly" (*VI* 142). When Alphonso Lingis describes the hundreds of bacteria inhabiting our mouths to neutralize plant toxins or those digesting the food in our intestines, he is extending this point to recent discoveries about the genetic and cellular makeup of our bodies which came long after Merleau-Ponty's death but which show that the symbiotic intertwinings within each organism do indeed mirror those outside those individual bodies. Mark Hansen explains that "specifically, [Merleau-Ponty's] conception of life as a transspatial emergence from the physiochemical introduces a fundamental correlation of behavior and morphogenesis that itself *grounds* the correlation of phenomenality and ontology."[52] At the same time, Merleau-Ponty's concepts of *écart* and dehiscence account for the distinctions among all creatures, unbridgeable differences among all living things that exist even as all are participating within the flesh of the world.[53]

In the *Nature* lectures, Merleau-Ponty was already recognizing biological continuism by considering the meaning of new work in evolutionary biology and discussing the silent emergence of humans and their horizontal relationship to other species that Teilhard had defined. Teilhard's analogy of human evolution to a flower emerging from a branch as a novel development from the form of a leaf is problematic in its reductionist linearity, as Gilles Deleuze and Félix Guattari might point out, for it ignores the "rhyzomatic" indeterminacy and multiplicity of relationships among living things.[54] But for Merleau-Ponty, the analogy provides a clear illustration of "the strange kinship" of humans and other animals, examined at the end of the previous chapter. Though he completely accepted that biological forms evolved over a period of many millions of years, he rejected what he saw as dogmatic and mechanistic Darwinian notions of mutation and natural selection that emphasize the activity of the environment on a basically passive organism (*N* 171, 175, 252). In doing so, he anticipated discoveries of our own time about evolutionary flexibility, genetic drift, and internal forces in organisms that are just as formative as external environmental constraints.[55]

The movement of topics and argumentation in Merleau-Ponty's exploration of animality in the 1957–1958 *Nature* lectures (second course) begins with what he called "The Tendencies of Modern Biology" in studies of embryonic development by Arnold Gesell and

G. E. Coghill, which move away from the rigid mechanical traditions of previous biology. Unlike deterministic Cartesian ideas of bodies as clearly defined assemblages of discrete working parts, the new biology examines the emergence of complex adult forms from simple beginnings that could never have formally predicted them or quantitatively produced them. Using the findings of such research, Merleau-Ponty shows how the development of the adult creature is organic, material behavior that is a kind of embodied meaning unfolding in participation with its environment. The gradual evolution of this organism from its completely different and rudimentary embryonic shape is a kind of echo within its body of the long evolutionary history of life on the planet. This is only an analogy or similarity, however, for Merleau-Ponty does not subscribe to Ernst Haekel's now-discredited claim that ontogeny recapitulates phylogeny. Rather, he implies that similar emergent forces are at work in both. The focus on embryonic growth and change works implicitly to prepare his audience for his later explicit emphasis on human evolutionary emergence from earlier forms. And in fact, the entire discussion of animality is interwoven with commentary on evolutionary concerns.

From embryology, the lectures go on to consider Jakob von Uexküll's innovative concept of the *Umwelt*, derived from careful scientific research on perception among many individual species, and then on to several ethologists studying animal appearance and formal mimicry. It culminates in a discussion of Konrad Lorenz's work on instinct. All along, as Merleau-Ponty moves to examine one example of research and then another, he is building a case for the profound interrelationship of creatures with their environments, from simple organisms to more and more complex ones and finally to our own species and the emergence of our particular way of "being a body" (*N* 208), with its distinctive consciousness, or what has been called "spirit" in traditional philosophy. This reflective quality of our being has emerged over evolutionary time from the immanent Logos or meaning of the biosphere as it too has changed from earliest life forms three or four billion years ago. Our consciousness is thus part of the profound biological continuity we share with other animals, as in the type of "pre-culture" Merleau-Ponty described in the behavior of crabs using shells of other creatures in a variety of ways, as we shall see later.[56]

At the heart of the animality lectures lies the assertion that "animality is the logos of the sensible world: an incorporated meaning" (N 166). This meaning is revealed in experiments on axolotl lizard embryos by G. E. Coghill in the 1920s and in work on human embryos by Arnold Gesell and Catherine Amatruda in the 1940s, in which development is seen to unfurl in behavior that anticipates the organism's future forms (N 144). The axolotl lizard begins its life as a tadpole living in water and gradually develops legs and moves onto land to grow into a seven-inch-long reptile. At first, it has no mobility but only muscles that can be excited locally by touch. At this stage, its motor system has no connection with its sensory system. Then, as nervous-system connections are made in the head, the organism can flex its head. From the head, the nervous-system connections move down the body to the tail, allowing first a stage of curling or buckling the body from head to tail and then uncurling and flexing in the other direction. Next the tadpole begins to make an S curvature to one side, in a wavelike movement across the body like a zigzag. When the animal makes several of these S movements from side to side, it is swimming. Coghill explains, "The development of anatomical connections is made in a temporal order, of such a kind that the movements and swimming are produced in virtue of the same embryonic development" (quoted in N 141). As the development continues, anterior feet begin to emerge but function within this global swimming behavior of the trunk. Their form anticipates their future function before there is any musculature to make them work independently, though "sketches of motor fibers" begin to appear in the feet. As Merleau-Ponty puts it, "The leg emerges, absolutely subjugated by the trunk, then it battles for its freedom" (N 142). Coghill is famous for introducing the idea that because the embryo is integrated and has moving gills in the egg well before the nervous system appears, the nervous system "is not the last explanation," or the central place or governing director of movement. Merleau-Ponty believes that the importance commonly assumed for the brain and nervous system comes from the easy way it fits with mechanical descriptions of the body. But the first behavior of the animal is organized "under preneural gradients [chemical, electrical, of temperature, etc.]; the nervous system emerges from a preneural dynamic" (*N* 142–143). In this way, the developing embryo is a dynamic system in profound participatory response to its surroundings.

Similarly, Gesell's work defines the animal body as "a take on the exterior world" whose organization is the same as behavior which is continually, dynamically reciprocal with that world. In another example of an animal body developing in order to properly interact with that world, he describes the premature human child, who has only a hesitant sleep that is difficult to distinguish from wakefulness, until organic development allows for the gradual development of two different behaviors that Merleau-Ponty explains are "reciprocal terms of a unique function. . . . Born or not, the child adheres to the internal sequence for the maturing of its behavior" (*N* 146–147).

As in the case of the axolotl feet, animal organs develop before there is a function for them. For example, the elements of the human electrocardiogram area appear in their adult state at nine and a half weeks of embryonic development, before there is any nervous control of the heart. Form thus anticipates function, carrying a reference to the future and embodying "a project in reference to the whole of [the creature's] life" (*N* 151). Gesell also described the way the elements of the embryo shift and shuffle into new positions and combinations, novel emerging parts and relationships. The stability of the organism is thus in constant flux, endlessly reshaping itself. For these reasons and others, Gesell insisted that "the organism is not a machine but a state of great dynamism" (quoted in *N* 150).

Earlier, Jakob von Uexküll had posited a *Bauplan* or implicit intrinsic building plan for each organism, which anticipated such embryonic research.[57] As we have seen, he had described the functioning of organisms within the particular environments, or *Umwelten*, created in reciprocity between their own perceptive abilities and the situations in which they are immersed. For each animal or plant, the surrounding habitat is full of "meaning factors" and "meaning carriers," things recognized in the subjective *Umwelt* that have significance as food or danger or opportunity according to the coherent functioning of the organism. "The life-task of the animal and the plant consists of utilizing the meaning-carriers and the meaning-factors, respectively, according to their particular building-plan." For Uexküll, "The question of meaning is . . . the crucial one to all living beings," and it is immanent in the world ("Theory of Meaning" 36–37; see also Hansen 251–254).

Uexküll's work is particularly important for Merleau-Ponty in its emphasis on the active role of all creatures in shaping their *Umwelten*.[58] This concept shapes an evolutionary understanding which he sees as fuller and less narrowly utilitarian than the popular Darwinian notion of ruthless environmental selection pressures determining which organisms are fit to survive. Instead, for Uexküll, the organism is equally active in shaping the environment in a coevolving situation. Merleau-Ponty shows how tautological the narrow Darwinian argument is.

> How do we understand this activity that shows an Umwelt? According to Darwinian thinking, there is nothing to understand. Different fortuitous elements are welded together because every other arrangement, or at least every bad arrangement, would not explain the survival of the animal. Only the animals that present extraordinary arrangements were able to survive. The factual conditions exclude every animal that does not present such dispositions. But this said, a Darwinian-type thinking suppresses the problem. We cannot show ourselves how this activity is constituted; we postulate that what is, is possible. Darwinian thinking gives the actual world the power to determine the only possible. (*N* 175)

The result is a Just-So Story or a Panglossian conclusion that whatever is, is right.

As a powerful alternative to such a theory, Uexküll's *Umwelt* concept accounts for the active behavior of the animal defining its territory in concert with the soils and plants and other organisms in its community and place, thus cocreating its world. We might think of an ant building its anthill with its fellows, changing the aspect of the place around it and enlisting other organisms such as aphids in feeding its community. Or we might point to the North American example of beaver ecologies that determined the landscapes of lakes and wetlands in the upper Midwest before European colonization. Corals around the globe make similar profound contributions to the reef systems that become home to a myriad of other animals and plants.

Such phenomena are not merely physical for Merleau-Ponty but also constitute symbolic and cultural behavior. Each animal, operating within its own *Umwelt*, Merleau-Ponty explains, "defines its territory as a privileged emplacement" and functions in a symbolic realm (*N* 176). A crab, for example, can use a sea anemone to camouflage its shell and protect it from predators or indeed to replace its shell if it has been lost, or it can use the sea anemone as food. "The architecture of symbols that the animal brings from its side thus defines within Nature a species of preculture. The *Umwelt* is less and less oriented toward a goal and more and more toward the interpretation of symbols" (*N* 176). This realm of meaning inheres in the relations among the parts of the organism, in the relations of the organism to its territory, and in the relations of animals among themselves, "so well that we no longer see where behavior begins and where mind ends" (*N* 178). Behavior must be motivated or orchestrated by some coherent force or tendencies, and the implication of this research suggests that mind or consciousness has evolved or emerged from tacit beginnings over millions of years, into more and more reflexive abilities in animals.

"What is thus unfurled?" asks Merleau-Ponty. "What is the 'subject' that Uexküll speaks of? The unfurling of the animal is like a pure wake that is related to no boat" (*N* 176). As Uexküll explained in 1909, the thing that is unfurled from the egg to the chicken is a chain of events that never becomes an object because its internal law never becomes visible to us. Instead we see only momentary manifestations that are always in the process of changing or even disappearing as some new shape takes over (*N* 176). Essentially this is not the manifestation of a new force, because the living creature works only with "physicochemical elements" in a spatial and temporal field where a "surging-forth of a privileged milieu" causes those elements to join according to unseen relations (*N* 177). Once this occurs, "We can at this moment speak of an animal," which is "like a quiet force" regulating, making detours, preserving its own inertia, as for example the planar worm does if it is cut in two, each part becoming a whole animal (*N* 177).

It would be difficult to find a more dramatic contrast between this sense of multiple, abundant, sentient agency and Heidegger's interpretation of Uexküll's *Umwelt* as a self-inhibiting ring that fundamentally captivates each animal, thus "withholding the possibility of the manifestness of beings" (Heidegger, *Fundamental* 258–259; see Bailly 49–50). We have seen that for Heidegger this means that nonhuman creatures cannot have genuine perception; they are "poor in world" (*Fundamental* 176–186). In contrast to that negative view, recent microbiological research has supported Uexküll's understanding of the active way that organisms shape their worlds, and information theory has extended the ideas about intrinsic meaning and kinds of communication which Merleau-Ponty drew from him. Richard Lewontin, for example, explains that "organisms not only determine what is relevant and create a set of physical relations among the relevant aspects of the outer world, but they are in a constant process of altering their environment." As they consume, organisms and living systems also produce; they are "the transformers of materials, taking in matter and energy in one form and passing it out in another that will be a resource for consumption for another species" (54–55; see also Rose 230–249). Indeed, "the *environment* is coded in the organisms' genes, since the activities of the organism construct the environment" (Lewontin 100).

From considering how animals create their *Umwelten* in interaction with their surroundings, Merleau-Ponty goes on to explore physical resemblances of animals such as butterflies or preying mantises or the Arctic fox to the environments in which they live. For him, the existence of the sense organ is similarly a kind of mystery, like the resemblance of the butterfly to its milieu, because it forms before it has anything to sense, as the butterfly forms before it knows what surroundings to adapt to. It is a physical history of relationship at the same time that it anticipates the world it will encounter.

In the final lectures on animality, Merleau-Ponty moves to consider the work of ethologists such as Niko Tinbergen and Konrad Lorenz regarding instinctive animal behaviors and their relation to language and sentience. As with his analysis of the embryological research of Coghill and Gesell, when discussing Lorenz, Merleau-Ponty emphasizes the way young animals anticipate future situations when they begin to behave in ways they have never seen others perform and for which they have no need as yet. These are fragmentary parts of not yet fully shaped or completed instinctive activities such as nest building which anticipate their futures. Lorenz gives the example of a young heron that will not build a nest until the following year but "one day perceives leaves, falls in front of them in a sort of ecstasy, then executes the behavioral stratagem of accumulation of leaves for the nest, and then falls back into calm. It is not that the instinct is yet there, but that it is announced by partial reactions. Then it is as if this behavior is erased." For Merleau-Ponty, "The instinct is an activity established from within but that possesses a blindness and does not know its object." It is thus not adaptation but anticipation of a possible situation (*N* 191–193). In a way, it is "a tension that wants to find relief without knowing why" and thus does not aim at the real as much as at something imaginary; it is a kind of drama that is closely related to symbolism that in reproductive rituals becomes "a phenomenon of reciprocal expression" (*N* 196–197). Lorenz sees mating behavior as coming close to human language, and his conclusions lead Merleau-Ponty to say that "we can speak in a valid way of an animal culture" (*N* 198; see Mazis 190–200). While Lorenz does not directly assert the existence of animal consciousness, Merleau-Ponty says that he "practically affirms that none of those who have a familiarity with animals would deny them consciousness." Merleau-Ponty responds to these speculations by concluding the animality lectures with what he sees as the basic question to be pursued: "Is there an animal consciousness, and if so, to what extent?" (*N* 199).

Merleau-Ponty died before he could go any further. But in fact, he had already implied the answer to his question throughout the animality lectures. In his discussion of the developing embryo's formal anticipation of its future, he described behavior as "a principle immanent to the organism itself," dynamically and tacitly shaping its emergence (*N* 145). This is a kind of tacit meaning which Uexküll called a *Bauplan* and which is central to his *Umwelt* theory. Merleau-Ponty writes, "The *Umwelt* is not presented in front of the animal like a goal; it is not present like an idea, but as a theme that haunts consciousness" (*N* 178). Similar to a dream, such a mode of knowledge is never self-conscious but is part of the relations among the parts of the organism, the relations of the organism to its milieu, and the relations among animals, constituting implicit meanings that emerge in "the higher animals" as instincts and various other kinds of consciousness. Given the way the discussion in the lectures moves from embryonic development in lizards and humans to research on a variety of insects and mammals, we can see that the evidence points to many kinds of animal consciousness, not simply "an animal consciousness." The extent and explicitness of such consciousness would have to vary widely. What Merleau-Ponty seems to have done is to set the groundwork for future theoretical analysis of research directly focused on particular animals and their ways of knowing the world. In the decades since his death, there has been a proliferation of such research, exploding in recent years into a revolution among ethologists and specialists in animal communication and cognitive neuroscience particularly applied to mammals. This research has confirmed Merleau-Ponty's emphasis on evolutionary continuism among living beings. Before we can look at a few examples, however, we must address some troubling aspects of his third course of lectures, of 1959–1960, "Nature and Logos: The Human Body," in which a certain tinge of human exceptionalism remains.

When Merleau-Ponty turned his attention to the human phenomenon that was the ultimate goal of his investigations of science and evolution, we find a special emphasis on what he occasionally called "soul" or "spirit," which he seemed to claim as uniquely human. At the beginning of this final series of lectures, he says he has moved from animality to the human body which issues from it during evolution. As intertwined with both animality and nature, humanity must first be understood "as another manner of being a body," with other living beings as variants of such intertwining (or *Ineinander*— "in another"; N 208). From this assertion, he proceeds to a discussion of the body as "animal of perceptions" (N 221) that gives rise to varieties of consciousness in the higher animals and then the unique human self-awareness that becomes Logos or Reason.

In the first lecture in this series, Merleau-Ponty asserts that "we are not animal," and he speaks also of the "strange anticipations or caricatures of the human in the animal" (N 209, 214). When discussing "the libidinal body and intercorporeity," he comments on the union of body and soul, speaking of the "Body of Spirit, nature of Spirit." He claims that its content is very different for humans than for animals and that the spirit or mind "is as natural to man as Nature is to animals" (N 224–225). Such distinctions seem to constitute a strange return to the traditional separation of humans from other animals, something like what Heidegger sought to capture with the concept of *Dasein*. When Merleau-Ponty explicitly discusses the place of humans and the human body in evolution, however, he accepts Teilhard de Chardin's insistence that there is no rupture in the evolutionary process, no point when we can clearly see humans emerge as a new form of life (N 267–268). As we saw in the previous chapter, Merleau-Ponty sees humans moving into their distinct form in a lateral kinship which remains with us. Thus he concludes that "animality and human being are given only together" (*N* 271). Only an understanding of our natal past as a species and our continued existence within "a fabric of preobjective, enveloping being" can give us an adequate sense of who we are; this is why his lectures "have given such a large place to the theory of evolution" (*N* 273).

Bryan Smyth insists that Merleau-Ponty's position "remains indelibly humanistic," even though Smyth sees it as potentially open to wider considerations of human-animal kinship.[59] But if we look at how Merleau-Ponty's description of human uniqueness is contextualized, I think we must conclude that he could not have meant that humans alone have consciousness or spirit. Glen Mazis explores the common ground between humans and other animals which Merleau-Ponty's writings on embodiment and his *Nature* lectures can suggest (21–48, 169–207). We have seen how Merleau-Ponty described the embodied meanings and movements toward culture and symbolism in the worlds of many other animals in the first two series of lectures, and how his discussion of the ability of our two hands to both touch and be touched in a sort of self-questioning of our body's flesh mirrors the kind of synergy that must exist among all creatures. Ted Toadvine concludes from carefully examining the whole body of Merleau-Ponty's philosophical writings that he "recognizes that our intertwining with animality requires a new understanding of reflection, . . . since treating the power of reflection as the distinguishing mark between humans and animals risks returning to a philosophy of consciousness that alienates humanity from life" (*Merleau-Ponty's Philosophy of Nature* 95–96). It is reasonable to suppose that in the *Nature* lectures Merleau-Ponty was still actively working out his thinking on the human place in the animal world and in nature more broadly and that he would have eventually acknowledged the continuum of various kinds of consciousness emerging through the evolution of myriad animal species. As I have already suggested, his commentary on Coghill's, Gesell's, Uexküll's, Tinbergen's, and Lorenz's research implies that animals have consciousness and their own *Umwelten*.

Indeed, in a short radio presentation about animal life which he gave in 1948, he criticized traditional mechanistic theories about animals and said that nonhuman animals "proceed to trace in their environment, by the way that they behave or act, their very own vision of things" and thus manifest "a kind of interiority."[60] The proliferation of animal studies in the decades since his death begins to show us in remarkable detail how this is the case with a wide range of other animals, from parrots to dolphins, dogs, and our cousins the great apes.

Until very recently, however, anyone wishing to study animal consciousness had to struggle against the twin problems of anthropomorphism and behaviorism. Skeptics charged that any description of animal thinking or intentional behavior could only be based on the sentimental projection of human qualities onto an unknowable Other. Behaviorists denied that even human psychological states could be known and therefore devised programs of mechanistic stimulus-response training that sought to eliminate complexity and train subjects with absolute objectivity. As Frans de Waal reminds us, the results of these latter regimens were appalling, crippling or even destroying normal development. In human orphanages and among nonhuman animals, illness and death were regular outcomes. John Watson and B. F. Skinner from the 1920s into the 1960s tried to convince parents to stop caressing their children or responding emotionally to them. Attitudes toward other animals were similarly focused only on conditioned behavior, and it was taboo to consider their inner life. "Animals were to be described as machines, and students of animal behavior were to develop a terminology devoid of human connotations," says de Waal.[61] Animal trainer Vicki Hearne tells us that with our own behavior, we get what we expect, often blocking the possibility of understanding other animals:

> To the extent that the behaviorist manages to deny any belief in the dog's potential for believing, intending, meaning, etc., there will be no flow of intention, meaning, believing, hoping going on. The dog may try to respond to the behaviorist, but

the behaviorist won't respond to the dog's response; there will be between them little or no space for the varied flexions of looped thoughts.[62]

Similarly, Nicholas Humphrey emphasizes the social aspect of intelligence and our access to it in other species by saying, "Indeed, I venture to suggest that if a rat's knowledge of the behaviour of other rats were to be limited to everything which behaviourists have discovered about rats to date, the rat would show so little understanding of its fellows that it would bungle disastrously every social interaction it engaged in."[63]

Fortunately, behaviorism and related charges of anthropomorphism are fading away as more and more species respond to serious interest in their ways of communicating among themselves and with other creatures, their social arrangements, and their many ways of intentionally manipulating their worlds (Griffin, *Animal Minds* 20–21). As Mary Midgley reminds us, "*all* our reasoning extrapolates from limited experience," including our understanding of the inner lives of other people (*Animals* 142). Because we evolved together with the other animals from simple microorganisms millions of years ago and have similar brain structures and organs and social habits, we can understand each other's behaviors and subjective states that are in many ways like our own (de Waal, *Ape* 41, 70).

De Waal comments on the fact that cultural biases of the kind we have been examining here and in the previous chapter have kept Western scientists from accepting the kinship of humans and other animals, particularly primates, and thus have delayed much crucial understanding of both ape behavior and its relation to humans, understanding that came much sooner for Japanese primatologists such as Kinji Imanishi. According to de Waal, Asian philosophical traditions have never set the human species apart from other creatures, so that the continuity among all life forms implied by evolutionary theory was willingly accepted by Japanese students of animal behavior (*Ape* 116). Indeed, after World War II, Japanese primatologists were the first to make the kinds of breakthroughs that we now take for granted, identifying such activities as deliberate teaching and learning between primate generations, invention of novel methods of preparing food, complex communication among individuals and groups of primates, and so on (*Ape* 117–119, 188–212). By contrast, the dominant forms of primate study in Europe and America in the first half of the twentieth century have been described by Donna Haraway as based in utilitarian laboratory situations dominated by rigidly disciplined experimental regimes predominantly focused on biomedical research. Unlike the Japanese, these Western experimental programs were often behaviorist and basically Cartesian, treating the animals as objects without meaningful emotional or intellectual lives. Haraway's description of the laboratories and the utilitarian arrangements for testing the bodies of thousands and thousands of monkeys and apes is horrifying from contemporary perspectives. The premises motivating this research were shaped by political and commercial trends, reflecting colonial practices especially in Africa, and by Cold War military concerns about aggression in humans and other animals (Haraway, *Primate Visions* 19–25, 115–123, 126–129). The field began to change in the 1960s and 1970s, however, with the entry of Japanese scientists into international conferences and the gradual and then quickly expanding practice of working with monkeys and apes in their natural environments. Haraway places special emphasis on the gender politics of these changes, analyzing the effect of the increasing involvement of women in this field work, beginning with Jane Goodall's pioneering chimpanzee studies in the Gombe region of Tanzania (*Primate Visions* 129–146). But de Waal points out that by the time Louis Leakey sent her out into the field, "the questions and techniques that would prove useful in this sort of endeavor had already been developed by Japanese primatologists, who had individually identified their monkeys and followed them long enough to understand the importance of kinship, the unexpected complexity of primate society, and the degree to which every group was different" (*Ape* 117, 188–189).

Leakey's role as the founding father-figure for this kind of research among Europeans and Americans may have been criticized by

Haraway as patronizing, deriving from a cultural habit of seeing women as closer to "nature" and more nurturing than men (*Primate Visions* 151–152), but from another perspective, it can be understood to derive also from his work with and appreciation of a gifted wife who was actually the person who discovered the bones of Zinjanthropus as well as protohuman footprints in the Olduvai Gorge. Because both Leakeys were concerned with the place of these early hominids in the evolutionary emergence of *Homo sapiens*, they naturally considered the great apes as our kindred and thus worthy of respectful approach within their own full environments. Once scientists moved out of their carefully controlled laboratory environments and into the rich and complex biosystems where primates live as they have for millions of years, radical changes were required in research methods and attitudes toward the animals. Chimpanzees, gorillas, and baboons, in the freedom of their jungle and savannah worlds, were not subject to scientific constraints or human coercion that limited their movements or behaviors. Instead the human researchers had to earn the trust of their subjects and learn to move along with them, behave within their codes of decorum, and understand their social lives and ordinary routines.[64] Modesty, respect, and restraint became critical for humans, who after all could be killed by their much stronger primate cousins. De Waal suggests that human-animal relationships must have been relatively egalitarian during most of our history for similar reasons, until domestication began to give us the illusion of superiority (*Ape* 63). This kind of research approach would thus be a return to long habits of thought only relatively recently displaced. In any case, they spread widely throughout animal studies as the twentieth century drew to a close, though the more instrumentalist laboratory experiments for commercial and biomedical purposes continued as well.

As a broader range of cross-species relationships developed, in which human researchers were situated within the worlds of the animals they were observing, more open attitudes about the animals have begun to motivate research, and remarkable insights have been emerging in both learned journals and television documentaries. No longer does human exceptionalism determine the kind of expectations Heidegger represented with his notions of "being with" world-poor animals. Instead the richness of many varieties of animal experience is being increasingly acknowledged and scientifically recorded, with ever more precise and nuanced questions asked and detailed findings established. Evidence for Uexküll's claims about overlapping *Umwelten* is increasingly available in the scientific literature, and the kinds of cross-species mirroring and exchange which Deleuze and Guattari called "becomings" are being described in greater and greater detail and frequency (Buchanan 151–186).

To conclude this chapter, let us turn to a selection of animal studies from the past few decades, to demonstrate how many of the supposedly distinctly "human" abilities now appear to be shared with animal kin of many species, thus bridging the supposed "abyssal" differences between us and demonstrating with more and more certainty the kind of biological continuism that genetic research also establishes conclusively but that Heidegger and so many of his followers refused to consider. Distinguished zoologist and founder of the field of cognitive ethology Donald Griffin recently surveyed the present state of animal cognition research in *Animal Minds: Beyond Cognition to Consciousness*. There he writes within the carefully disciplined scientific style typical of scholarly journals and books, refusing to come to any conclusions unsupported by definitive evidence. Even the question of whether scientists have demonstrated that animals are conscious is answered by "not yet" because of the difficulty of gathering incontrovertible quantifiable, "objective" evidence. "Have scientists proved conclusively that animals are never conscious," he asks, "perhaps by means of evidence so complex and technical (like quantum mechanics) that ordinary people cannot understand it?" (x). No is also the answer to that question. Griffin cites several kinds of valid evidence that bear on the question, however, from animal communication to intentional manipulation of the environment, to tool manufacture and use, to cognitive neuroscience showing similar neural mechanisms for learning and memory across species (xi–xiv). Some examples may be familiar to the general public from television documentaries and media reports, such as the bonobo Kanzi, who communicates with people using a keyboard of lexigrams, or Alex the African grey parrot, who could count, do simple mathematics, and identify colors and shapes. Scientists such as Jane Goodall, Alison Jolly, Frans de Waal, Irene Pepperberg, and Michael Tomasello have written books in a more popular vein about their research with particular animals. These books for lay audiences are thoroughly documented by specialized academic research.

Griffin devotes almost an entire chapter to the communicative dances of honeybees, which have been carefully and ingeniously studied since Karl von Frisch's discoveries from the 1920s through the 1940s about how their waggle dances and round dances signal the distances and locations of food sources. In chapter 3, we shall see how other kinds of communication have recently been discovered among bees and some other social insects (*Animal Minds* 192–194). Scientists have had to invent techniques for recognizing and describing the behavior of these insects, whose physical structures and behaviors are so different from our own and those of other mammals. Griffin remarks that "honeybees are quite versatile, and perhaps we have underestimated their cognitive abilities" (191). Their learning ability rivals that of mammals in some studies, with particular complex aspects of learning in rats and pigeons also found in honeybees in work by such scientists as Mark Bitterman, Patricia Shinoda, Charles Lee, Margaret Couvillon, and others in the 1990s.

The most obvious way to learn about animal cognition would be through language, but until recently only human forms of communication were dignified with that term. We will save that vexed subject for the next chapter, but here it can be understood that many ingenious methods have been found to explore the ways other animals communicate among themselves without benefit of our kind of language. Like Nicholas Humphrey, Mary Midgley places particular emphasis on social arrangements as indicators of cognitive complexity and intentional activity, arguing that social animals must interact together if they are to survive. "Such animals need, not just to notice behaviour, but to attribute motives in order to interpret it. For this they must rely on their own feeling" (*Animals* 141). De Waal agrees that animals can display intentional social actions based on understanding of emotional states of others, discussing the complex grooming behaviors of chimpanzees and the sexual activities of bonobos that are used to diffuse antagonistic feelings among group members, to forge alliances, to comfort aggrieved individuals, and so on (*Age of Empathy* 84–117). Heidegger's claim that apes do not have hands that can share and welcome and give, communicating complex thoughts, is clearly ridiculous when seen in the context of such primate studies and widely available documentaries about chimpanzees, bonobos, gorillas, orangutans, and baboons.

Pepperberg understood the crucial role of social relationships among intelligent birds and decided at the outset of her research with Alex that she would need a social form of learning closer to the way wild parrots learn. She used a method developed by German ethologist Dietmar Todt, in which one trainer (A) is the model for the animal subject and its rival for the attention of a second trainer (B) who ask questions back and forth about the names of objects. Because of Alex's relationship with Pepperberg and her assistant, he learned by watching this social interaction with remarkable speed not achieved by previous direct forms of training. Pepperberg explains, "The stronger the relationship, the more efficient the learning, just as with children."[65]

Such social relationships were long ago seen by Japanese primatologists to constitute cultural transmission of information passed on from one generation to later ones, as they were able to demonstrate with the surprising discovery in 1953 of the invention of a technique of washing sweet potatoes in a freshwater stream on the island of Koshima by an eighteen-month-old female macaque monkey named Imo. Notified of this behavior by a farmer's wife on the island, Imanishi and his students studied the macaques on the island and documented the spread of this behavior along kinship lines among the juveniles and females, which resulted in three-quarters of the population adopting it within five years. Imo also introduced the additional innovation of washing rice that had been thrown on the beach, putting it in sea water so that the rice floated and any sand around it sank. Then retrieving the clean rice was simple. That technique also was eventually adopted by most monkeys on the island. Many years after these events, de Waal visited Koshima and witnessed these behaviors among a population born long after Imo's relatives had adopted them. By this time, they had also learned to eat fish discarded by human fishermen (*Ape* 200–204).

Other cultural behaviors discussed by de Waal include paintings by chimpanzees that manifest symmetrical coverage of a canvas, rhythmical variations, and vivid color contrasts. Evidence from many examples of painting apes shows that they "have a sense of both balance and completeness, enjoy the visual effect of what they do, and create regularities and patterns, but are not out to produce a lasting product" (*Ape* 167–173). In *Animal Minds*, Griffin also comments on aesthetic activities among animals, particularly apes (243) and bowerbirds (96–99). Bowerbirds offer an intriguing example because they are not mammals close to humans as the great apes are. Building their bowers as courtship displays designed to attract females, male birds take two years or more to learn the techniques necessary for creating attractive structures, with local and individual patterns of decoration that are learned manifestations of cultural styles. These also demonstrate conscious thought by the individual birds about what they are building (98–99).[66]

Wolfgang Kohler in 1917, Jane Goodall in the 1960s, and many others more recently have documented tool use among chimpanzees, bonobos, and orangutans (de Waal, *Ape* 243). Though the use of straws or twigs for fishing termites out of their mounds is the classic instance noticed by Goodall, de Waal comments in particular on the more complex and difficult use of stones for cracking extremely hard nuts in West Africa, which has been noted in scientific journals since 1951 but well documented by primatologists only since the late 1970s. Chimpanzees in Bossou, Guiana, were found to use particular cracking sites for a very long time, and the techniques involved take years for young chimps to learn by observing their elders. De Waal reports that human villagers in the area use exactly the same technique to open the same nuts, with identical cracking tools, except that those of the humans are somewhat lighter (*Ape* 240–241). Indeed, evidence has been found of chimpanzees using such technology for more than four thousand years.[67] Griffin reports tool use among animals from insects to many species of birds, as well as mammals such as sea otters and of course primates and elephants (*Animal Minds* 113–121).

Griffin also surveys widespread construction of artifacts by groups such as ants and beavers alongside such intentional shaping of tools for specific purposes by individuals. Well-known examples are ants shaping pitfall traps for prey, mollusks and crabs digging burrows, bees constructing hives, birds and primates making nests (*Animal Minds* 80–99), and beavers building elaborate dams that create entire ecosystems. Scientists have carefully documented the skillful adaptation of these animals' technologies to function in locations that are never identical and that are often changed by such forces as weather and stream flow to require ingenious repair. In spite of skepticism that these activities could result from intentional thought, Griffin describes the ways that beavers must evaluate particular sloping banks in order to choose workable sites for dams and burrows, the ways they select the trees to cut for their constructions, and many examples of the adaptation of building techniques to the circumstances of flowing water and mud consistency as they construct their dwellings and dams and shape pieces of wood to fit exactly where holes or leaks need to be plugged (*Animal Minds* 103–112). Such widespread behaviors among a significant variety of species show us that animals build in order to dwell in significant locations about which they think and intentionally adapt culturally transmitted habits to the particular demands of a stream needing damming or a web needing to fit a specific space or a nest in a particular tree or a hive in a newly inhabited cavity (see Ingold 172–188). Heidegger was mistaken to think that such building, dwelling, and thinking are reserved for one kind of primate in the family of *hominidae* that includes chimpanzees and bonobos, or even just for primates.

Indeed, Montaigne's and Darwin's assertions that many animals share abilities and mental and emotional states with our species are finding more and more support in animal studies of all kinds. De Waal tells the story of a mischievous chimpanzee named Georgia who was fond of filling her mouth with water and sneaking up on unsuspecting human visitors in order to spray water on them. One day when he saw her sneaking up on him, he looked her straight in the eye and pointed at her, warning in Dutch that he had seen her. Though she probably did not know that language, she stepped back at once, let some of the water dribble out of her mouth, and swallowed the rest. For de Waal, Georgia's behavior makes most sense if described as resulting from clear social awareness, intentions to surprise, and a sense of mischief (*Ape* 66). It is hard not to see a sense of humor in such behavior, and a clear intention to deceive. Griffith gives numerous other examples of deceptive behavior among animals, from fireflies, shrimps, and birds to vervet monkeys (*Animal Minds* 212–227). Now we have ample scientific research demonstrating that elephants and many other mammals have complex emotions similar to our own, grieving for dead family members, manifesting joy at reunions, indeed all the kinds of responses which pet owners report from ordinary experience with them.

Similar responses can be observed in many kinds of birds, but some recent studies have shown remarkable intellectual abilities as well, including mathematical concepts and precise memory of hundreds of hidden nuts, for example, by Clark's nutcrackers.[68] Irene Pepperberg was able to teach Alex simple mathematical skills such as counting, but he developed the concept of zero by himself without her help (191–193). This is particularly significant because the concept of zero was not a part of European mathematics until after importation from Arabic mathematicians in the twelfth century. Such examples indicate that animals have intellectual powers and ways of knowing far beyond unaided human abilities. Scientific studies are proliferating on how dolphins and whales use sonar in the sea to navigate, bats use echolocation to find their way and hunt their prey, and elephants hear through their feet.[69] Such recent discoveries ought to chasten human assumptions about our species superiority and to open us to respecting the many ways our animal kin are rich in world in different registers and styles from our own.

Our ancestors from the Pleistocene through the Mesolithic and Neolithic periods revered the powers of the many other creatures among whom they lived, as the cave paintings in southern France make clear and as thousands of other visual records testify on ancient petroglyphs and frescoes from the Mongolian Altai to caves in South Africa and rock faces all over the Americas. Francis Pryor speculates that gathering and hunting peoples moved with the herds of herbivores and birds around them in seasonal patterns, gradually developing methods of tracking and herding them with dogs, in behaviors still evident in the cooperation of shepherds and their dogs in contemporary Britain.[70] He suggests that during the fifth millennium BCE, "we see a gradual switch to loose herding, followed by close herding towards the Later Neolithic and Early Bronze Age," with dogs probably assisting them (125). Such behaviors required richly sensitive and complex cross-species awareness, communication, and interaction. I myself witnessed some of these relationships in one of the few surviving hunting and gathering cultures, the Hadzabe people of Tanzania, whose dogs help them to hunt the wild animals such as gazelles, antelopes, and guinea fowl which make up a significant part of their diet.[71] We have not really come very far from the way of life of these contemporaries who offer a glimpse of how humans lived for thousands of years before they invented the wheel and gunpowder and set themselves on an illusory throne above their animal kin. Nicholas Humphrey describes in witty and playful terms the long evolutionary journey we have taken together, as sensation began to emerge from the self-protective reactions of the simplest early organisms, developing into more mediated perceptions and finally self-consciousness among some mammals and birds. He describes

> how present-day sensory activities could have developed step by step from primitive beginnings: starting with a local

"wriggle of acceptance or rejection" in response to stimulation at the body surface, later a sensory response mediated by nerves traveling from the body surface to the brain and back again, later still a progressive short-circuiting of this loop by the targeting of the response not on the body surface as such but on the incoming sensory nerve, and eventually the emergence in higher animals of sensory-reverberating feedback loops within the brain.[72]

In the next chapter, we shall see how these shared developments and abilities in the animal community of our planet produced a proliferation of languages we are finally relearning to hear.

CHAPTER

3

Language Is Everywhere

Language is central to being human. From Descartes to Heidegger and most contemporary Western philosophers, language and its connection to rationality have defined the transcendent Logos that is supposed to distinguish our species.[1] Merleau-Ponty spent his life attempting to dismantle that dualistic view. "The only *Logos* that pre-exists is the world itself," he said in *Phenomenology of Perception* (lxxxiv). He insisted that we are embodied creatures caught up in a world that is full of meaning and language. For him, "the whole landscape is overrun with words," and the task of philosophy is to recapture "a birth of meaning, or a wild meaning, an expression of experience by experience, which in particular clarifies the special domain of language" (*VI* 153). He never directly addressed the question of whether other animals possess language or reason as philosophers might describe those capacities, but his acceptance of an evolutionary continuum of living beings, his description of incipient cultures even in the activities of such animals as crabs, and his consideration of animal consciousness suggest that he might well have done so if he had lived to complete his projected description of the "man-animality *intertwining*" in the world. We have seen in the previous chapter how his late work sought to investigate some of the ways biological research supports Jakob von Uexküll's description of the meaningfulness of living creatures' relationships with their environments. Uexküll implies widespread communication throughout the natural world with his emphasis on "meaning factors" and "meaning carriers" that exist for living beings in the habitats surrounding them. It takes only a step or two of inference to see that if this is true, dynamic relational behaviors within those habitats are analogous to signaling and receiving signals. Similarly, creatures' relations with each other involve transmissions of meaning, as they reach out and reciprocate in bodily gestures of cooperation or conflict, courtship, nurturing, or signaling danger or the presence of food.[2] Such an understanding is consistent with Merleau-Ponty's chiasmic ontology and seems to be assumed in his explicit treatments of human language. For him, the meanings which we find in the world are lifted by "our acts of ideation" from an underlying or surrounding brute being that is dynamic and mysterious; we have to continually return to their wild state to rediscover those meanings (*VI* 110). "The Intertwining—The Chiasm" chapter of *The Visible and the Invisible* opens by suggesting the need to rediscover "within the exercise of seeing and speaking some of the living references that assign them such a destiny in language" (*VI* 130). The chapter concludes with the claim that the whole landscape is overrun with words and echoes Valéry's notion that "language is everything, since it is the voice of no one, since it is the very voice of the things, the waves, and the forests" (*VI* 155).

Merleau-Ponty's linguistic theories point toward the emergence of language in humans from bodily structures and behaviors shared with many other animals, and recent animal language studies as well as work in the evolution of language strongly support that theoretical position.[3] George Lakoff and Mark Johnson's view that language arises from metaphorical expressions of physical experience offers a contemporary development of Merleau-Ponty's embodied approach to language.[4] Sympathetic echoes of his broader claim about the omnipresence of language in the world appear in the more recent field of biosemiotics that developed from Uexküll's work and makes connections among biological sciences, linguistics, and cultural studies to explore communication and signification in living systems. Wendy Wheeler argues that biosemiotics offers a new way of understanding the development of human language as "an evolutionary accomplishment in which the semiosis that is apparent in all nature achieves a new, and more complex, level of articulation."[5] This way of thinking can be extended to an understanding of literature's place in the living community, where it functions as one of our species's ways of singing the world to ourselves, in concert with the songs and artistic creations of many other creatures, from birds and primates to dogs and dolphins.

This chapter takes a position within debates about animal language, asserting that human linguistic behavior gradually emerged in the course of evolution from neural structures and physical behaviors we share with primates and other animals, that it remains embedded within shared abilities and cultures in a continuum of animal behaviors that are themselves part of a myriad of communications in the living world, and that increasing evidence suggests that it is embodied and gestural, as Merleau-Ponty claimed more than a half century ago. Once a heretical or at least marginal opinion among philosophers, scientists, and linguists, such a view is gaining adherents, in part because of Sue Savage-Rumbaugh's work with chimpanzees and bonobos, Irene Pepperberg's work with her African grey parrot Alex, new findings about elephant communication, and increasingly sophisticated studies of whale and dolphin communication. But strenuous objections continue to be raised against the possibility that other animals have semiotic communication or can be taught to interact in linguistically significant ways with humans. To engage these debates, we must first confront the vexed question of what constitutes language and adopt a definition that makes sense in terms of cognitive linguistics and neuroscience, as well as evolution. Using this definition, we will examine some of the most significant recent studies by animal language scientists and the counterclaims of their detractors before moving to survey recent work on the evolution of human language.

After examining the majority view among recent researchers from many disciplines that human linguistic capacities function within an evolutionary continuum of cognitive and communicative behavior among animals, we will move on to see how Merleau-Ponty's writings about language anticipated such findings. We will explore his work on the basic gestural, embodied quality of language, his description of language acquisition in children, and the relation of that work to what we have learned about linguistic behavior in other animals. From this perspective, it seems increasingly clear that many creatures have ways of "singing the world," in Merleau-Ponty's terms, through a range of physical performances and creative activities that are in effect different kinds of art. Merleau-Ponty's description of literary art can be understood as a human production within the vast array of "languages" suffusing the world, rendering visible or audible many of the hidden meanings experienced by living beings within their distinctive *Umwelten*. The final section of the chapter examines a representative example of a literary effort to gesture toward or include the semiotic behaviors of other animals.

To begin, we must confront the problem of what counts as language. I shall be using a broad sense of the term that includes a range of communicative, semiotic behaviors in humans as well as, potentially, among many other animals. Typically, when a previously unknown communicative ability is discovered in an animal community, skeptics rush to discount its validity by detailing ways in which it differs from human language in complexity of syntax, creativity, or indication of independent agency. A classic example is the waggle dances of honeybees, whose communicative functions were described by Karl von Frisch from the 1920s through the 1940s and have been carefully studied by other scientists since that time. Obviously bees do not speak in voices like ours, and their methods of signaling information are very different from human gestures. Yet as Donald Griffin explains, in spite of some remaining skepticism, it now seems quite certain that bees and some other social insects such as ants communicate to nestmates various kinds of information about food sources, possible dangerous intruders, and locations of possible new homes for swarms. Inside the hive, communication occurs through odors and ingesting behaviors to indicate whether more nectar is needed or whether pollen or water are required instead (*Animal Minds* 192–194).[6] The discoveries of Savage-Rumbaugh about the linguistic abilities of the bonobo Kanzi are much easier to accept as related to human language, though she too has faced skeptical arguments from scholars who demand evidence of grammatical structures and category formation like those in human language.[7] Because Kanzi was raised among humans and surrounded by speech as young children are, he learned to understand spoken English and to respond using a keyboard of symbols. He can understand a complex range of sentence types and create statements of syntactic complexity and novelty to express his desires, plans, memories, and activities (Savage-Rumbaugh, "Bringing Up Kanzi" 64–69). He also talks to himself by using the keyboard with his back turned to human companions or by moving to a place where he thinks the symbols he is touching are not visible to observers. Sometimes Savage-Rumbaugh could tell that he was thinking to himself about plans to misbehave, which he later carried out (52). His ability to comprehend is similar to that of a two-and-a half-year-old human child, though his ability to produce language is limited by the number of symbols on his keyboard and the time it takes him to search among them to find what he wants to say (69, 73). Even with the rich body of evidence such research has produced, skeptics continue to deny genuine linguistic status even for Kanzi's abilities and those of other species such as elephants, whales, and dolphins that have intricate communication systems that scientists are only just beginning to recognize or "hear."[8]

Cognitive neuroscience makes it impossible to define language in narrow anthropocentric terms based on logic and human communication. Instead we need a practical definition that accords with what we know about the evolution and structure of the brain and about the embodied quality of thought and language. Such a concept of language would account for the membership of human language among the complex communication systems of many animals. As Derrida said,

> The idea according to which man is the only speaking being, in its traditional form or in its Heideggerian form, seems to me at

once undisplaceable and highly problematic. Of course, if one defines language in such a way that it is reserved for what we call man, what is there to say? But if one reinscribes language in a network of possibilities that do not merely encompass it but mark it irreducibly from the inside, everything changes. . . . And what I am proposing here should allow us to take into account scientific knowledge about the complexity of "animal languages," genetic coding, all forms of marking within which the so-called human language, as original as it might be, does not allow us to "cut" once and for all where we would like to cut.[9]

It is easy to keep changing the definition of language to exclude modes not exactly like our own. Philip Armstrong describes how this process has characterized recent debates on ape language potential, so that when cognitive abilities formerly considered uniquely human seem to be possible for apes such as Kanzi or Koko, criteria are changed, the bar raised higher. "Once the [American Sign Language] experiments established that apes could use symbolic representation, the debate shifted to whether they could master grammar; when they showed they could manipulate syntax, scientists asked whether they could achieve 'cross-modal matching,'" and so on.[10] Now researchers such as Derek Penn, Keith Holyoak, and Daniel Povinelli insist that in order to have language, apes must not simply reason by association or social context but according to higher levels of logical abstraction, and they must base their linguistic activities on a theory of mind for those with whom they communicate. These scientists claim that only humans can reinterpret the "perceptually grounded representations" that a number of other animals can also understand, raising them to "higher-order, role-governed, inferentially systematic, explicitly structural relations" which are the flexibly adaptive logical abstractions familiar in mathematics and other human symbolic systems (109–178).[11]

Such a description of how the human mind works is mistaken, according to neuroscientist Antonio Damasio. In *Descartes'*

Error: Emotion, Reason, and the Human Brain, Damasio explains that commonsense ideas about pure abstract concepts in mathematics and other symbolic systems are fictions. Many people share the false intuition that all our perceptions and concepts occur as if on a large movie screen in a single brain structure or activity, a sort of "Cartesian theater."[12] But actually what we commonly assume to be abstract concepts are constructed as perceptual images resulting from "complex processes operating behind the scenes, in numerous regions of the cerebral cortex and of neuron nuclei beneath the cortex, in basal ganglia, brain stem, and elsewhere" (Damasio 96–98). These processes are sensory, shared with many other animal species, and involve ancient as well as more recently evolved brain structures associated with primal emotions and motor activities (108–113). They form our cognitive unconscious, by definition not accessible to self-reflection. Furthermore, they are dynamic and transitory, just like our sense of self, which is being constructed from moment to moment, "so continuously and consistently *re*constructed that the owner never knows it is being *re*made unless something goes wrong with the remaking" (240). We never have an understanding of some absolute reality outside ourselves (97); rather, as we saw Uexküll suggesting in his *Umwelt* theory in the previous chapter, we "know" only what our particular sensory abilities allow us to perceive about the world around us. We cannot hear ranges of sound that dogs or elephants or whales can hear; we cannot practice echolocation as bats and dolphins do; we cannot see in the dark as cats and other nocturnal creatures do.

In addition to being based on mistakes about how the human mind actually works, the exclusion of all but the most abstract human cognitive and linguistic behaviors from the definition of language is not very useful in view of what we are learning about other animals' communicative abilities. In their own wild environments, primates and wolves, elephants and lions, crows and parrots make their ways through complex and always changing environments to survive dangers, to find food, and to reproduce, maintaining intricate social relationships that have gone on for thousands or even millions of years. An openness to finding other linguistic modes than human ones could surprise us if a variety of scientific efforts continue to be applied to animal communication. According to Sue Savage-Rumbaugh and Duane M. Rumbaugh, "Animal language may be expressed in media apart from vocalizations and gestures; it may use natural materials, such as vegetation, to communicate topics that are germane to the cohesiveness of the community."[13] Indeed, Victor Norris suggests that even bacteria can communicate by a nonchemical form of signaling and that similar signals might be used by neurons in the brain.[14]

Without going into the continuing debates among scientists over continuity or discontinuity among species, or observational and relational rather than strictly reductionist experimental programs in laboratories, or what counts as "real science," we can say at present that communicative behaviors developed with mammalian species and that they are deeply social in their origins and intertwined with dynamic participation in rich physical environments. Scientific methodologies should therefore be set up to examine linguistic behavior in situations that adequately embody the full social and environmental complexities in which nonhuman animals live. Rigidly Cartesian, reductionist laboratory experiments fail to do this in the same way that rat mazes fail to capture the circumstances of normal rodent functioning in the world (Griffin, *Animal Minds* 254; Armstrong 207–208). The results of such experiments are just as intellectually impoverished as the situations designed to produce the evidence, as Merleau-Ponty himself asserted (*World of Perception* 58).[15] Cary Wolfe cites Humberto Maturana and Francisco Varela's view that animals equipped with signifying repertoires "develop their ability to participate in linguistic domains in proportion to their interpersonal interactions with other languaging beings" but that if deprived of rich environments of linguistic and relational behavior, their behaviors become more mechanical and limited.[16] This is much the same point Vicki Hearne makes about the failures of behaviorists as dog trainers (see previous chapter). Stuart Shanker defines a middle ground among the various competing approaches which offers a practical stage for moving forward. For him, "What is so interesting about the research on Kanzi and Panbanisha are the things which the Cartesian dismisses. What matters most is not what they cannot do, but what they can; and more precisely, the factors that enable these (latent?) capacities to flourish."[17] No one would deny the distinctive linguistic abilities of humans, from the complexities of our verbal behavior to the invention of writing and all that it has made possible. But the evolutionary continuum in language development increasingly established by work in many disciplines shows human cultural and linguistic activities to be vitally embedded in the living world, as John Dewey said long ago.[18] We share linguistic and aesthetic relationships with other animals in what Merleau-Ponty calls intertwinings or chiasms. Humans have always been involved in cross-species communication and cooperation, as exemplified by ancient practices such as sheep herding with dogs, horse riding, riding and using elephants for heavy lifting tasks, and domestication of goats and yaks and water buffalos.

At this point, however, we should try to account for how our particular primate branch began to develop its present array of languages between one hundred thousand and fifty thousand years ago. Christine Kenneally explains that after one hundred years of philosophical and scientific refusal to consider the evolution of language, the subject has recently opened up with discoveries in paleoarchaeology, cognitive neuroscience, evolutionary genetics, linguistics, and the kinds of animal studies we have been discussing. Interdisciplinary cooperation among these fields now supports the view that "human language lies on a continuum that includes other human abilities and the abilities of non-human animals" and that it took some six million years to coevolve with and then differentiate from common mammalian traits (149; see also Johnson 149). Whenever it happened and whatever the stages of its emergence might have been, the majority view among researchers at present is that distinctive human speech and cognition developed gradually out of gesture and the kinds of primitive vocalizations we shared with other primates, taking on distinctive forms in a kind of codevelopment with the creation of flaked tools, cooperative foraging and hunting activities, and cultural behaviors such as painting and sculpture and music (Kenneally 122–141, 188). We developed the ability to vocalize in ways primates cannot because of changes in the position of the larynx and tongue over time and because of cognitive differences.[19] Kanzi's or Alex the parrot's abilities to use English are thus not the same as human language, but it seems obvious that both animals have learned to communicate, using our linguistic tools in rudimentary ways documented by extensive scientific observation.

Philip Lieberman cites research demonstrating that the eventual ability to understand precise meanings is not a matter of simple word recognition. Instead more complex cognitive activity is required, involving brain centers for shape and color perception, vision, and motor activities, as well as acoustic recognition and processing. Humans share most of these brain processes with other creatures, from frogs to apes and dogs. Human speech involves complex patterns of format frequencies that can be perceived by many other animals as well, including some birds, apes, and dogs. It consists of highly encoded signals in which individual consonants and words are not perceived as discrete items analogous to beads on a string but instead as interrelated elements that determine each other in context. Acoustic cues for a consonant, for example, are "spread across an entire syllable and merged with the acoustic signal that conveyed the vowel" (Lieberman 93, 100–101, 126–127). Understanding speech thus requires complex perceptive and interpretive abilities, not just recognition of particular words. Dogs understand many human words and phrases and their emotional colorings, and they come to do so by being bathed in language, much as human infants do, in relational, emotive contexts where they work with their whole bodies to participate in meaningful behaviors, as Merleau-Ponty explained in *Consciousness and the Acquisition of Language*, as we shall see, and as Mark Johnson more recently describes according to increasing experimental evidence (34–45). Indeed, Lieberman cites brain imaging research showing that cortical areas homologous to those activated in humans during the production and reception of speech are also activated in chimpanzees and dogs that understand human language (36–37).

The relatively new field of biosemiotics helps to theorize a wider understanding of language by making connections among biological sciences, linguistics, and cultural studies to focus on communication and signification in living systems. This discipline grew out of Uexküll's *Umwelt* theory, the work of Charles Sanders Peirce on linguistics, and Thomas Sebeok's creation of the subfield of zoosemiotics. Danish biologist Jesper Hoffmeyer asserts that the essence of the entire life process is semiosis. "The most pronounced feature of organic evolution is not the creation of a multiplicity of amazing morphological structures, but the general expansion of 'semiotic freedom,' that is to say the increase in richness or 'depth' of meaning that can be communicated: From pheromones to birdsong and from antibodies to Japanese ceremonies of welcome" (*Signs* 61). He introduces the term "semiosphere" to identify the dimension or sphere that he claims suffuses the atmosphere, hydrosphere, and biosphere, "incorporating all forms of communication: sounds, smells, movements, colors, shapes, electrical fields, thermal radiation, waves of all kinds, chemical signals, touching, and so on. In short, *signs* of life" (*Signs* vii, my emphasis). Because our ecological awareness is still focused on the physicochemical level of energy currents, biomass, and food chains, he believes we have overlooked this intricate network of meaningful relations in which all organisms participate by sensing significations that are crucial to their flourishing. The discipline of biosemiotics attempts to remedy this omission and to create bridges among scientific disciplines with their very different methodologies, while allowing a restoration of communication with disciplines concerned with cultural history and ethics (viii). Uexküll's *Umwelt* theory is important to Hoffmeyer's reasoning, because it restores agency to organisms which conventional Darwinian thinking seems to have lost, with its fixation on natural selection and random mutation, forces operating on essentially passive organisms. We may recall that Merleau-Ponty made a similar criticism of Darwinian thinking in his *Nature* lectures. Uexküll might seem to have been reactionary in his refusal to accept the idea of evolution because of its emphasis on randomness and lack of design, but leading biologists of our own day have similarly criticized the Neo-Darwinist focus on passive creatures at the mercy of random forces from the external environment and internal forces of mutation that are entirely mechanical and outside their control. Hoffmeyer cites Richard Levins and Richard Lewontin as having pointed out that organisms actively move from one environment to another in search of favorable conditions for survival. The locust is one dramatic example provided by Hoffmeyer, in which a grasshopper under certain conditions changes its anatomy and its behavior in response to climatic stress, forming enormous hordes in a kind of locust superorganism that devours everything in its path. Levins and Lewontin also stress the way all organisms actively shape their environments in exchanges that affect physical surroundings and the lives of other creatures around them (Hoffmeyer, *Signs* 55–57). For Hoffmeyer, Uexküll's attention to the subjective realms of living organisms and his insistence on the meaningfulness of their interactions with the world around them provides a crucial explanatory function for evolutionary biology, even though he was not able to see it in his own lifetime. This perspective opens the way for a recognition of the semiotic dynamism of the biosphere.

In *The Whole Creature*, Wendy Wheeler draws from biosemiotics, as well as from complexity theory and Raymond Williams's appeal to evolutionary science in *The Long Revolution*, to agree with Hoffmeyer's assertion of the semiotic nature of all life. Wheeler believes that a paradigm shift is under way in science, philosophy, and cultural studies to recognize that "articulate language" is an evolutionary accomplishment bringing the semiosis apparent in all nature to a more complex level (14–21, 120). Any fruitful definition of language has to set human linguistic behavior in this wider context in which meaning codes and communication are everywhere in the living world, even on as minuscule a scale as DNA-RNA messages, enzyme reactions, neural linkages, and hormonal effects. Such interchanges and messages also appear in the electronic and chemical emissions of plants and their responses to abiotic forces such as sun and rain.[20]

As we have seen, Merleau-Ponty began to anticipate such ideas in the *Nature* lectures, examining particular scientific research from the 1920s to the 1940s to show how meaning and a kind of protoculture exist throughout the natural world. But these investigations late in his career were preceded by extensive work in psychology and in child development, whose linguistic dimensions found expression in the chapter of *Phenomenology of Perception* called "The Body as Expression, and Speech" and in lecture courses in Lyon and Paris during the late 1940s. The *Consciousness and the Acquisition of Language* lectures of 1949–1950 at the Sorbonne represent the most mature development of these courses on language.[21] Later, in *The Visible and the Invisible*, written during the same period as the *Nature* lectures, Merleau-Ponty extended his consideration of language more broadly into his chiasmic vision of the human place in the world and his consideration of how literary works function to render invisible meaning accessible. His ideas are congruent in many ways with what animal language studies are demonstrating about communication among many other creatures and with biosemiotics. Indeed, Hoffmeyer acknowledges his debt to Merleau-Ponty's phenomenological philosophy in his discussion of the relation of subjectivity to temporality and to the self-reference and noncoincidence that characterize all living systems.[22]

The core of Merleau-Ponty's linguistic philosophy appears as part of his work on embodiment in *Phenomenology of Perception*. There he defined human speech as essentially gestural, part of our physical life rather than belonging to some disembodied activity of mind. Indeed, he said that "the body is a natural power of expression" (*PP* 187). Thought is therefore not the representation of some preexisting idea but is constituted simultaneously with expression. In speaking and thinking, we behave according to an order we do not consciously know, full of sedimented meanings created by speakers before us. We are able to speak only

> by donning already available significations, which are the results of previous acts of expression. The available significations suddenly intertwine according to an unknown law, and once and for all a new cultural being has begun to exist. Thought and expression are thus constituted simultaneously, when our cultural assets are mobilized in the service of this unknown law, just as our body suddenly lends itself to a new gesture in the acquisition of habit. Speech is a genuine gesture and, just like all gestures, speech too contains its own sense. (*PP* 189)

In other words, "I understand the other person through my body, just as I perceive 'things' through my body. The sense of the gesture thus 'understood' is not behind the gesture, it merges with the structure of the world that the gesture sketches out and that I take up for myself" (*PP* 191–192). Speaking subjects share a common gestural world in the evolving biosphere and have their origin within "a primordial silence." They are part of a dynamic cultural texture that has been passed on from one generation to another for thousands of years.[23] Merleau-Ponty saw the conventional and seemingly arbitrary nature of present linguistic behaviors as relatively late developments in this process and as presupposing earlier means of communication. If we took the full emotional, gestural aspects of language into account, he claims, "It would then be found that the words, vowels, and phonemes are so many ways of 'singing' the world" (*PP* 193).[24] The many specific human languages are various ways for the human body to sing the world and live it, and that is why "the *full* sense of a language is never translatable into another" (*PP* 193). Each language in its own way expresses its unique cultural experience and understanding of the world.

The individual human infant develops language by being bathed in such gestural and auditory behavior from the moment of birth. In *Consciousness and the Acquisition of Language*, Merleau-Ponty explains that the polymorphous and spontaneous babbling of all infants during the first months of life is the ancestor of language in the developing individual. It emerges simultaneously with gestures and facial expressions such as smiles in response to the facial expressions and other body language of adults who are gazing at the child, touching it, and interacting with it verbally in dynamic interrelations that gradually develop into mimicry (Merleau-Ponty, *Consciousness* 11–13).[25] Even the nursing infant in the first months of life laughs and smiles in satisfaction and in answer to the smiles of those around it. This very early relational behavior is the context from which language will emerge (12).[26] Speech addressed to the infant excites it, and this acoustic sensation in turn stimulates its limbs and phonotory organs (14). In Merleau-Ponty's view, we make use of our bodies as *"a way of systematically* going toward objects" (35), and this means that the young child is working with its whole body to participate in the surrounding linguistic activity.[27] The child is enticed by the style of the surrounding language "until a single meaning emerges from the whole," because meaning "is immanent to living speech as it is immanent to the gestures by which we point out objects" (51).

Sue Savage-Rumbaugh describes a similar situation as having given rise to Kanzi's ability to communicate with lexigrams representing English words and phrases. Kanzi learned both spoken language and the meanings of the lexigrams by simply being with his mother, Matata, from infancy for more than two years, as Savage-Rumbaugh worked with her using a kind of systematic linguistic instruction previously adopted for chimpanzees. Matata was not learning very successfully, but unbeknownst to the experimenters, Kanzi was spontaneously absorbing the meaning of the lessons as human children do, just by being immersed in the linguistically rich situations around him. When Kanzi was old enough for Matata to be taken away for mating, he suddenly began using the lexigrams to communicate with his human caregivers. His ability far surpassed his mother's or that of the chimpanzees Sherman and Austin, with whom Savage-Rumbaugh had previously had limited success.

From that point on, Kanzi learned new lexigrams and gestures rapidly, gaining an impressive capacity for understanding and responding to spoken language ("Bringing Up Kanzi" 22–27).[28] A similar progression happened with his younger sister Panbanisha and other bonobos who were raised in linguistically rich environments as young children are. The breakthrough achieved by this research seems to correspond with Merleau-Ponty's description of the profoundly social and cultural aspects of language emergence in children, which grows out of the bodily, gestural experiences of relationships with adults around them. In the case of Savage-Rumbaugh and her fellow researchers' work with Matata, Kanzi, and other young bonobos, the infants of another species grew up in a mixed linguistic environment including both bonobo gestural communication and human gestural as well as vocal communication. The humans learned to interpret and use bonobo gestures from Matata and young Kanzi, and they simultaneously taught many human gestures to their ape coparticipants in daily interactions as Kanzi grew older and learned to communicate his desires to play or go to a particular place or eat a treat he could see but not reach ("Bringing Up Kanzi" 55–57). Thus body language shared across species made a bridge with human linguistic activity, and continuing daily social activities built trusting and cooperative relationships which nourished the linguistic development of the bonobos and led to the emergence of their use of lexigrams and comprehension of human speech (see Greenspan and Shanker 195).

Merleau-Ponty's description of infant language acquisition and cognitive development as requiring the kind of emotionally intersubjective, reciprocal gesturing in intimate social relationships of touching, gesturing, and mirroring or imitating facial expressions and body movements clearly also applies to intellectual and communicative development among the great apes and could well apply in other registers and degrees to animals such as dogs, horses, and elephants. Indeed, Vinciane Despret makes a convincing case for similar reciprocity in the relationship between the famous horse Clever Hans and his human handler, suggesting that Hans helped to shape the collaboration that resulted in his correct answers to mathematical problems, his spelling of words, and his discrimination among colors and musical tones. "The practice was not on the questioner's side only: Hans was teaching them what made him move. Hans the horse was as much leading them as the humans were leading him" (116).[29] Such profound bodily interrelationship and cross-species communication must be the result of very ancient habits of cooperation that coevolved with prey and predator relationships many thousands of years ago. In the case of hunting with dogs and the herding practices that grew from it, these relationships developed gradually from the Paleolithic era, fifty thousand years ago or even earlier, through the Mesolithic stage between the Ice Ages and the postglacial periods to the Neolithic era of plant and animal domestication of ten thousand or so years ago.[30] The domestication of horses is more recent, but it can be traced back six thousand years in central Europe.[31] Such relationships are evidence of protolinguistic behaviors among many mammals emerging from the primordial silence posited by Merleau-Ponty as the realm where meaning and expression originate. We have already seen some of the ways he used the *Nature* lectures to explore meaningful behaviors and cultures in creatures far different from mammals, from anticipatory development in ontogenesis to the "reciprocal expression" embodied in ritualistic behaviors discussed by Lorenz and Tinbergen (*N* 198; see also Toadvine, *Merleau-Ponty's Philosophy of Nature* 89). But it is in *The Visible and the Invisible* that he extended the embodied, gestural definition of speech from the earlier works into an ontological description of language bubbling up from silence and reaching back into the Invisible to articulate meanings that are the lining and depth of the sensible world. Here we continue to see the speaking word dynamically woven into the texture of social life with all its cultural accumulations, in a chiasmic overlapping with the visible world.

For Merleau-Ponty, the human body is a nexus in a web of significations woven throughout a world full of immanent meaning. The immense history of the earth's existence is sedimented beneath its surface but here and there revealed in geological uplifts or uncovered by scientists in cores drilled from ancient ocean beds or depths of Arctic ice. The past two centuries of comparative animal studies, genetics, and microbiology have shown how our individual bodies manifest a parallel intersection and overlapping of evolutionary development and kinship. Now, as Jesper Hoffmeyer explains, research has offered ample support for Darwin's assumption that interpretive activity of organisms is required for natural selection. Recent work on microRNAs and their key role in gene regulation make it clear that

> it is the lineage—seen as a historical and transgenerational subject—that acts as the selective agent via its overall reproductive patterns. By virtue of the genetic specifications carried forward from generation to generation by individual organisms, the lineage maintains—and continuously updates—a selective memory (the momentary pool of genomes) of its past that in most cases will be a suitable tool for producing individuals capable of dealing with the future.[32]

Merleau-Ponty describes a reversibility by which we can coil back on ourselves and look at that sedimented history. Because my body is made of the same flesh as the world and is one of the visible things, "this flesh of my body is shared by the world, the world *reflects* it, encroaches upon it and it encroaches upon the world. . . . They are in a relation of transgression or of overlapping" ("Working Notes," in *VI* 248–249). The concrete experience of seeing oneself in a mirror is accompanied by an imminent, invisible sense of oneself as perceiving; thus the visible reversibility terminates in the invisible realm of significance. A parallel reversibility allows us to hear and feel the invisible sounds within us that others can hear: "Like crystal, like metal and many other substances, I am a sonorous being, but I hear my own vibration from within; as Malraux said, I hear myself with my throat" (*VI* 144).

Human language intensifies this coiling back of self-reflection by allowing us to articulate the meanings we find sedimented in our experience, as language is itself a long cultural accumulation of significations, and "even the cultural rests on the polymorphism of the wild Being" (*VI* 253). All creatures with voices articulate their sedimented experiences in ways we only faintly understand. Hoffmeyer describes such sedimented meanings and communicative interactions existing even within embryonic cells, whose "positional history" stretches back over innumerable generations of cells and determines "choices" those cells make in the unfolding development of the embryonic organism (*Signs* 81). Merleau-Ponty did not live to explore these varieties of linguistic behavior, but he implied their existence. He said that the effort of articulation "is the Being of every being" (*VI* 127) and spoke of particular "constituted" human languages as certain regions in the universe of significations (*VI* 118). As we saw in the previous chapter, he thought the kind of synergy within our body must also exist among different organisms; it follows that this synergy must include the regions in the universe of significations shaped by the articulations of all the other creatures. From the rasping of cicadas to the songs of whales and birds to the howling of wolves and the vocalizations of primates, the world is full of voices. Christine Kenneally describes "a huge, shining network" of linguistic threads connecting all the speakers of one language to each other and weaving an invisible pulsing web of human languages covering the earth (3). If we use the broader working definition of language proposed earlier in this chapter, we see that network as much more vast than Kenneally's description, for it includes the myriad communication systems of all living creatures (see Norris 397–405). Glen Mazis explains that if we consider other creatures' ways of "languaging" within their particular contexts and manners of being, we will come to understand how they achieve "their own distinctive excellence" in communicating (92).

Such a formulation takes liberties with Merleau-Ponty's linguistic considerations in *The Visible and the Invisible*, but only by following directions he had set in motion in the *Nature* lectures as well as in the implications discussed earlier. What is true of languages applies also to cultures. If there are protocultures even among crabs, then the much more elaborate patterns of migration and courtship display and educational behaviors of many birds and mammals come even closer to human cultures. Thus Merleau-Ponty's commentary on the communication among human cultures can extend to those of other animals as well and can account for the existence of continued dynamic interchanges across species for millions of years as they coevolved on the planet. He asserted that "the communication from one constituted culture to another occurs through the wild region wherein they all have originated" (*VI* 115), and such an emphasis on wildness—like his frequent references to the Brute being that underlies all life and is our only environment—seems necessarily to draw in the cultures of the many animals with whom we are laterally related through our evolutionary histories. Ted Toadvine concludes that for Merleau-Ponty, "animal being is, therefore, just as much as human being, an interrogative fold within the world's flesh" (*Merleau-Ponty's Philosophy of Nature* 96). Indeed, Merleau-Ponty included other animal bodies than ours as both perceiving and being perceptible to themselves: "All depends, in short, upon the fact that it is the lot of living bodies to close upon the world and become seeing, touching bodies which (since we could not possibly touch or see without being capable of touching or seeing ourselves) are *a fortiori* perceptible to themselves."[33] The other animals like us are therefore "experiences, that is, thoughts that feel behind themselves the weight of the space, the time, the very Being they think, and which . . . [therefore] have about themselves a time and a space that exist by piling up, by proliferation, by encroachment, by promiscuity—a perpetual pregnancy, perpetual parturition, generativity and generality, brute essence and brute existence, which are the nodes and antinodes of the same ontological vibration" (*VI* 115).

In human speaking and the development of writing, our cultures have found a way of catching some of this pregnancy and vibration in the mesh of self-reflexive articulation. Each of us enters into this texture of linguistic culture as an infant awakening out of silence by babbling and interacting with our caregivers, gradually participating in a "language-thing" that is a formal part of the phenomenal world and lies at the heart of literature and philosophy.

> [If] we consider the speaking word, the assuming of the conventions of his native language as something natural by him who lives within that language, the folding over within him of the visible and the lived experience upon language, and of language upon the visible and the lived experience, the exchanges between the articulations of his mute language and those of his speech, finally that operative language which has no need to be translated into significations and thoughts, that language-thing which counts as an arm, as action, as offense and as seduction because it brings to the surface all the deep-rooted relations of the lived experience wherein it takes its form, and which is the language of life and of action but also that of literature and of poetry—then this logos is an absolutely universal theme, it is the theme of philosophy. (*VI* 126)

This description does not explain how the language of the spoken word moves into the written word of literature and philosophy; that is the question to which we shall now turn.

Merleau-Ponty describes our ideas as thoughts that have a future in us by forming in conjunction with speech and breaking through our space of consciousness to be shared with the others who hear it and thus to have a future with them. Finally, "having become a writing, [such a thought] has a future in every possible reader, [and] this can be only that thought that leaves me with my hunger and leaves them with their hunger" (*VI* 118–119). This is authentic speech that is fresh, not "too much possessed" like a cliché or common formula or dead metaphor, and it catches up those around us in a dynamic web of shared expression and ideas we cocreate.

> Whether he speaks up or hardly whispers, each one speaks with all that he is, with his "ideas," but also with his obsessions, his secret history which the others suddenly lay bare by

> formulating them as ideas. Life becomes ideas and the ideas return to life, each is caught up in the vortex in which he first committed only measured stakes, each is led on by what he said and the response he received, led on by his own thought of which he is no longer the sole speaker. No one thinks any more, everyone speaks, all live and gesticulate within Being, as I stir within my landscape, guided by gradients of differences to be observed or to be reduced if I wish to remain here or to go yonder. (*VI* 119)

This living process of discussion can be put into writing by one person, with others reading and responding on pages which still others will read. Such "discussions" stretch out over time and space, involving groups of readers never imagined by previous writers, as my responses to Merleau-Ponty's writings are intertwined with those of animal scientists and poets and cognitive neuroscientists from many countries. All become part of unfolding conversations which are long cultural gesticulations within the being of our species entangled in the myriad lives of the biosystems that sustain us.

The operation of what Merleau-Ponty calls "aesthetic expression" in *Phenomenology of Perception* is distinctive in that it "confers an existence in itself upon what it expresses, installs it in nature as a perceived thing accessible to everyone, or inversely rips the signs themselves—the actor's person, the painter's colors and canvas—from their empirical existence and steals them away to another world" (*PP* 188). Later, in *The Visible and the Invisible*, he links this unique power to the proper language of philosophy and emphasizes its openness to mystery and its power to disrupt ordinary expectations, in other words to defamiliarize the world so that we see it afresh and glimpse some of the relations between the visible and "the interior armature which it manifests and which it conceals" (*VI* 149). The object of philosophy, like that of poetry, is not to try to hold things "as with forceps, or to immobilize them as under the objective of a microscope, but to let them be and to witness their continued being." It is a matter of opening energetically on Being, in order to "more closely convey the life of the whole and make our habitual evidences vibrate until they disjoin" (*VI* 101–102). This kind of writing does not foreclose but instead leaves us with our hunger and yearning. That is because "we ourselves are one sole continued question, a perpetual enterprise of taking our bearings on the constellations of the world, and of taking the bearings of the things on our dimensions" (*VI* 103). Science is equally engaged in this enterprise, but its methods are different, focused on precision and certainty which must necessarily be reductive of the complexities of the world and thus forestall continued questioning in shaping second-order systems of explanation.

For Merleau-Ponty, the most difficult point about the power of language is its capacity to reveal "the bond between the flesh and the idea, between the visible and the interior armature which it manifests and which it conceals," and he finds Marcel Proust an exemplar "in describing an idea that is not the contrary of the sensible, that is its lining and its depth" (*VI* 149). Literature, music, and painting explore this bond as nothing else can. Aesthetic works cannot be detached from the living dynamism of the world and be erected as "a second positivity" of explicit denotations as scientific ideas can. Instead they remain untranslatable experiences of the mysteries they have implied or embodied. What Proust says of musical ideas such as Swann's "little phrase" which recalls his love affair with Odette applies to all "cultural beings" or works of art. They embody "unknown forces" and "laws" whose secrecy we experience and tacitly understand as we understand our carnal experience. But they are at once present *and* disguised or "veiled with shadows." To try to make them explicit "does not give us the idea itself; it is but a second version of it, a more manageable derivative," like any reduction to five written notes of the musical phrase that is so evocative in Swann's actual hearing and memory (*VI* 150). The work of art as experienced in its first contact or vision and pleasure is an initiation—"the opening of a dimension that can never again be closed" (*VI* 151). In this way, it bears us off to another world as we hear the music or see the painting or read the novel or poem. It is the transforming of primordial silence into speech. A writer or musician or painter creating a fresh work is a gesture and its meaning a glimpse of the invisible world of secret folds within the reality we can see.

Because Merleau-Ponty died before he could elaborate these ideas in the final section of his project, we do not know the terms by which he would explain how literary works "gesture" and thus open these dimensions that can never be closed, how Proust for example uses words to convey the complex meanings Swann finds in the little musical phrase. It is not by simple mimesis, not by some naïve representation or naming. In Merleau-Ponty's last working note, written in March 1961, he said that the second section of his ontological project, Nature, is "a description of the man-animality *intertwining*" and that the third section, Logos, would not "take Logos and truth in the sense of the Word" but rather be "a study of the language that has man." It is what is realized in man "but nowise as his *property*" (*VI* 274). What I have been suggesting is that this language is the human voicing of immanent meanings in the world, what Merleau-Ponty elsewhere called "the deep-rooted relations of the lived experience, . . . the language of life and of action" that bubbles up out of our mute experience of primordial silence, "the most valuable witness to Being" that we can achieve (*VI* 126). And my particular point is that literary works achieve this witnessing within a larger network of animal articulations, which Merleau-Ponty barely hinted at but which are implied by his continual emphasis on man-animality intertwining, on the yearning for articulation of every being, and on the profound synergies that link living creatures together on the planet. Human efforts are part of a larger tapestry of animal expression and aesthetic creation.[34]

Other animals surely also have ways of perceiving and communicating realities that are not obviously tangible or visible to us. Animals' alarm calls heralding the coming of earthquakes might be an example of such singing the world. Communication among migrating birds and butterflies participates in similar "natural magic" that Merleau-Ponty defines as intrinsic to speech. Donald Griffin, working from a scientific background in animal studies, suggested as early as 1977 that "it is now thinkable that communication with animals might eventually be developed to the point that it could be used to obtain from them simple but nevertheless significant introspective reports if, contrary to prevailing opinion, they have mental experiences and are capable of conscious intentions."[35] He describes a gradually increasing willingness among his colleagues to accept such work as beaver dams, spider webs, and bowerbirds' bowers as aesthetic creations. Literature is the recorded creation of such culturally evolved meanings for humans, and it is one of our distinct ways of singing the world to each other. Some writers, such as Virginia Woolf and Yann Martel, have attempted to describe our complex intercommunications with other animals. Elsewhere I have discussed Woolf's fictional evocation of the interplay of human and other animal languages and behaviors (Westling, "Virginia Woolf"). For present purposes, Martel offers a more recent meditation on cross-species communication in his novel *Life of Pi*, one that I believe speaks to the increasing planetary danger of catastrophic climate change and species extinction.[36]

Philip Armstrong sees *Life of Pi* as one of a number of recent novels depicting "ubiquitous images of a diminished and fragile world," which late in the twentieth century suddenly began to replace previous faith "in the boundlessness of non-human nature" (5). He agrees with Randy Malamud's interpretation of zoos as grotesque prisons where animals are objects of perverse human voyeurism and control, removing them from their rich natural ecosystems and destroying their capacities for agency (174–175).[37] Thus he reads Martel's novel quite negatively as a zoo story that reinforces Enlightenment attitudes about animals and values of scientific modernity. Armstrong also charges Martel with a tourist mentality typical of late capitalism, which motivates his emphasis on Pi Patel's attempt at synthesizing the major world religions in his view of the sacramental nature of the world. Pi "collects faiths like souvenirs," says Armstrong, and his "affection for zoos as embodiments of the wonder of nature, and his comparison of captive animals with hotel guests, suggest the superficial perspective of the transient visitor" (179). Some of this criticism is apt, particularly regarding Pi's condescending attitudes about the animals in his father's zoo. Malamud's examination of the history of zoos destroys any possibility of accepting Pi's comfortable assumptions, but it could be argued that the novel itself places these in an increasingly ironic context as the narrative develops. Martel's treatment of the major world religions need not be seen so negatively, however; Pi shares the desire to respect and value the great religious traditions with many serious theologians and spiritual people all over the world in this era of murderous sectarian violence and dogmatism. In any case, I believe that Armstrong's caveats can coexist with an appreciation for Martel's insistence on confronting the fact of human domination of other animals for thousands of years. What has changed recently in that long relationship is the vastly increased reach of our species's global impact, so that in certain ways, all other life is now threatened by human behavior and the attitudes that propel it. The spaces on the planet where wild animals can live freely are shrinking dramatically every day, so that it can almost be said that they themselves are only large zoos, increasingly threatened by encroaching logging, mining, agricultural, and military forces.

I read Martel's unlikely shipwreck tale as an apocalyptic allegory of cross-species communication and uneasy cooperation for survival on a vastly diminished planet. If we accept animal trainer and poet Vicki Hearne's definition of language games created by animal training, Ludwig Wittgenstein's question of whether we could understand a lion if he spoke is answered in a limited way in Martel's novel, because a human and a tiger learn to understand each other through gesture and symbolic event, though not through human speech.

Life of Pi works to challenge the human exceptionalism of Western philosophical tradition by dramatizing exactly how constrained we are by physical needs that coevolved on this planet with all the other living things that must kill and eat each other. Using a lifeboat as an elegant material pun on what the earth is for us, Martel strips down the circumstances of his main characters to minimal conditions for mammalian life.[38] The lifeboat is simultaneously an ark that provides the chance of survival for an absurd cargo—a sixteen-year-old boy with the name of a swimming pool (another irony, given where he is stranded) and an adult Bengal tiger named Richard Parker. The novel functions as a conceit for the diminished remains of the planet's living community, struggling to keep alive after mass extinction. Piscine Molitor Patel is an unlikely Noah, the son of a zookeeper who realizes that he must continue in his father's profession if he does not want to become the final meal for Richard Parker. Pi's musings and strategies are meditation and practice within the necessary discipline of animal training that humans have used for at least ten thousand years to dominate predators and thus at least temporarily to win an evolutionary competition for survival.

We remember that in *The Animal That Therefore I Am* Derrida questions the gaze of a very different kind of cat—his small pet—on his naked body, acknowledging, "in such moments of nakedness, under the gaze of the animal, everything can happen to me, I am like a child ready for the apocalypse" (12). We have noted in chapter 2 how Derrida insists on respect and acknowledgment for the many different kinds of animal others and wonders whether they can respond to us. Vicki Hearne answers in the affirmative, moving far beyond Derrida's tentative deconstructions with a searching application of Wittgenstein's and Stanley Cavell's thought, interwoven with vivid examples of training disciplines that allow humans and horses and dogs to perform intricate dances of cooperation. Yes, animals respond. Trainers always talk about animals as moral agents and active partners in performances of reciprocity that are a kind of conversation. We may not be able fully to understand a lion's language, nor he ours, but we can learn to understand body language of other animals, as scientists such as Jane Goodall, Dian Fossey, Barbara Smuts, Frans de Waal, Michael Tomasello, Duane Rumbaugh, and Sue Savage-Rumbaugh have shown. Throughout our species's existence—as well as through the prior coevolution that produced *Homo sapiens*—we have carefully observed and interwoven our lives with them. Merleau-Ponty's description of the bodily, gestural nature of human language helps us see that we have never ceased to participate in the network of animal languages throughout the living community.

Maurice Merleau-Ponty's chiasmic ontology suggests the best ground for understanding the situation, but its benign generality must be complicated and made more specific to include the violent and terrible bloodiness of animal interrelationships within the messy mutability of the flesh of our world. As we have seen, his ontological position in *The Visible and the Invisible* emphasizes our immersion in wild or brute being and our synergy with other creatures. The *Nature* lectures were heading away from humanism as they probed the philosophical implications of evolutionary biology and ethology, describing a lateral rather than a hierarchical relation of humans and other animals, a "moving beyond [*dépassement*] that does not abolish kinship."[39] Martel's *Life of Pi* explores Merleau-Ponty's "man-animality intertwining" in a radically minimalist situation—a kind of Samuel Beckett adventure at sea. This happens in the second half of the book, during which the cast of characters is quickly whittled down to only two—the massive predator and the puny human who must devise a method of taming him enough to last through their voyage. Because Richard Parker is a wild animal, however, he will never be domesticated into an ally or trusted companion. As Vicki Hearne says of chimpanzees and wolves, he will never invest himself in human society as a domestic cat or dog or horse will do (22–23). Richard Parker will remain fiercely, terrifyingly Other. Pi Patel has to devise ways to dominate the tiger, to turn the lifeboat into a zoo, and to keep his charge fed and watered for 227 days.

A Hindu from birth who has embraced the benign principles of all the major world religions, Pi must become a predator and change his eating habits to acknowledge the bloody economy of killing and eating other creatures that defines earthly life. Donna Haraway insists in *When Species Meet*, "There is no category or strategy that removes one from killing. Killing sentient animals is killing someone, not something; knowing this is not the end but the beginning of serious accountability inside worldly complexities" (106). That, I believe, is Martel's position in imagining the disaster that traps Pi and the tiger on the lifeboat. Pi learns how to use the boat and its equipment most skillfully to navigate through storms and to provide food and water for himself and Richard Parker. In reciprocity, Richard Parker, following his own wild directives, at one crucial moment also saves Pi from death. Each must learn to read the other; each must adapt his behavior and linguistic habits to allow mutual communication. However, the boundary between them is always fragile, and the terrain of overlap (or the demilitarized zone between their *Umwelten*) remains small.

Or perhaps the novel is really only about human animality. I will come back to that possibility a little later.

The opening half of *Life of Pi* is a prelude to the desperate situation of the castaway boy and tiger of the second half. This prelude thinks back to Pi's happy childhood in Pondicherry and considers relations between himself and the animals in his father's zoo. In describing this place, Pi seeks to refute common deprecations of zoos as prisons where animals are turned into objects for the gaze of urban humans. Graham Huggan sees Martel's position as based on a respect for the radical otherness of wild animals whose lives are shaped by predation.[40] "Well-meaning but misinformed people think animals in the wild are 'happy' because they are 'free,'" Pi explains, but wild animals lead lives of compulsion and necessity within an unforgiving social hierarchy in an environment where "the supply of fear is high and the supply of food low and where territory must constantly be defended and parasites forever endured" (Martel 15–16). The zoo, by contrast, satisfies each animal's basic needs for food and safety in a comfortable territory analogous to a human house (18). It may be, in fact, that after what humans have done to the planet, zoos are the only place where remaining wildlife can ultimately survive (19). Pi's father takes pains to ensure that his sons understand the terrifying otherness and danger of zoo animals, in spite of their apparent placid natures in their zoo enclosures. He takes his family to watch as a goat is placed in the cage of a tiger who has not been fed for three days. After that spectacle, he lists all the horrible ways that creatures from sloth bears to deer, hyenas, and ostriches can kill a human. "Life will defend itself no matter how small it is," says Pi's father. "Every animal is ferocious and dangerous. It may not kill you, but it will certainly injure you" (38). This is the distinction Hearne makes in her discussion of the chimpanzee Washoe, who despite her ability to use American Sign Language for communication with people remained so physically dangerous and unpredictable in maturity that she had to be restrained with chains and cattle prods to take a walk with human companions (18–41). Pi comes to understand the distinction between wild and tame under the direst possible circumstances.

The crisis occurs as Pi's family is traveling aboard a Japanese freighter carrying a variety of their zoo animals to a new home in Canada. One night in a storm, the ship breaks apart, and Pi finds himself on a lifeboat among a motley group of survivors that includes a zebra with a broken leg, a hyena, an orangutan, and the Bengal tiger named Richard Parker. In only a few days, Richard Parker has dispatched all but Pi, in a spectacle of suffering and slaughter among individuals whose emotions Pi observes closely and understands. The plight of the orangutan Orange Juice is particularly moving, because Pi has known her for many years and sees her as almost human. But finally there he is, trapped on the twenty-six-foot boat with the powerful tiger who soon will digest his previous meals and will need more flesh (137).

Martel is remarkably clever in making the situation plausible and in playing it out with convincing detail for more than one hundred pages, as Pi learns how to cope with his circumstances and lives through many weather events and fishing adventures, training Richard Parker to accept his authority and keeping them both fed. The fascination of the *techne* involved here has the same kind of appeal we find in *Robinson Crusoe* and the *Swiss Family Robinson*. But for our purposes, it is the psychological and linguistic dynamics of Pi's relationship with Richard Parker that matter, suggesting some of the ways Martel seeks to explore the importance and power of human engagement with kindred animals.

Pi's unavoidable relationship with the tiger necessitates some form of communication and the invention of arrangements that allow the two to share the space of the lifeboat (164). In order to avoid being killed, the boy comes to realize that he has to train the tiger to respect him. Such authority would have to be based on his understanding of tiger social rules and earned by stimulating common animal emotions of fear and submissiveness. Having observed Richard Parker's queasiness during rough seas, Pi initiates a regimen using the lifeboat's emergency whistle while violently rocking the boat to induce seasickness. The tiger learns to associate the whistle with nausea and thus to submit to the human who is also the only source of food and water. In this respect, however, Pi is like any other zookeeper or guardian of domestic animals in that he is the servant as well as the master of his charge. A minimal common language emerges from propinquity and the training regimen. This language is contextual and bodily, involving both human and tiger vocalizations as well as actions such as the direct stare (162–164, 207, 222–223). As mentioned previously, Hearne explains this kind of process by adapting Wittgenstein's notion of language games to the discipline of dog and horse training and describing the dance of embodied communication between species that results. Her work supports Merleau-Ponty's description of human language as deeply gestural, intimately intertwined in a network of relationships with other creatures and forces articulating the world's immanent Logos. Similarly, Cary Wolfe speaks of Derrida's "insistence on the fundamentally ahuman character of language, its erosion by its other, by *all its others*: 'as we human beings exist in language,' with our bodyhood functioning as 'the system of nodes of operational intersection'" with the world.[41]

In spite of Pi's dominance in this little world, he soon understands that he is an animal much like the tiger. He eats the same way Richard Parker does, with "noisy, frantic, unchewing wolfingdown" of raw flesh (Martel 225) and sees that together they are "two emaciated mammals, parched and starving" (239). Furthermore, in a strange, dreamlike Samuel Beckett encounter with another lifeboat manned by a starving cook, Pi learns how bloodthirsty humans become when desperate. The cook tries to kill and eat Pi, but the tiger springs out and eats the cook instead.

Finally the tiger and the boy reach land, and their relationship is severed, each reverting to his separate way of life. Pi reacts with sadness, because Richard Parker has meant so much to him as the only companion in his grief and his struggle for survival. Richard Parker, however, true to his wild nature, does not even look back as he fades into the jungle.

The novel's appendix offers an alternative ending to the story, when Pi describes the representatives of the Japanese shipping company who come to hear his testimony about the fate of their ship and refuse to believe that he and a tiger could have survived together. Finally Pi sighs, "You want a story that won't surprise you. . . . You want a story without animals." "Yes!" exclaim the Japanese interviewers (303). So Pi tells a different story, in which he and his mother, the cook, and a sailor with a broken leg survive. The cook first eats the sailor, then Pi's mother. Finally Pi kills the cook and eats him. This alternative story is less interesting, but in the shadow of the drama of boy and tiger, it makes a similar point about human animality. Which one shall we believe? If Richard Parker is only another human, most of Pi's strategies for survival are unnecessary, Martel's long meditation on human relations with other animals is empty, and the narrative is only a clever cheat.

Graham Huggan and Helen Tiffin emphasize the way Martel plays here with traditional attitudes toward animals, complicating the trope of their wild nonhuman bestiality and their alternative use as allegorical figures for human descent into savagery. For Huggan and Tiffin, the two radically different stories of the voyage serve to destabilize conventional species boundaries and to playfully blur the distinction between cannibalism and ordinary carnivorous feeding.[42] Indeed, even boundaries between plants and animals are contested in the strange episode of the floating algae island, which has a place only in the main story of Pi and the tiger with the human name. Here Pi and Richard Parker find temporary refuge on what seems an idyllic floating community of closely interwoven, large green algae forming a matted landscape of some twenty miles in circumference, with trees sprouting up as extensions of the tubular algae and mysterious ponds of fresh water dotted all over the island. Hundreds of thousands of meerkats are the only inhabitants of the island, and they become easy prey for Richard Parker, while Pi contents himself with algae for food. Both revel in the deep ponds of fresh water and gradually regain their strength. A horrible secret lies at the heart of this island, however, which the meerkats and the tiger understand in part because of the burning in their feet caused by walking on the surface of the algae at night. The meerkats always retreat into the trees to sleep, and Richard Parker returns almost desperately to the lifeboat every night, licking his paws. Pi has slept in the boat at first but then establishes a hammock in a tree for safety. Only when he tests his foot on the "ground" one evening does he learn that the algae releases a seething acid at night that "eats" mammalian flesh and that it does the same to the bodies of fish that stray into the freshwater ponds created by the algae. The whole island is carnivorous. In a large tree at the island's center, Pi finds a hideous fruit that looks benign and green at first but turns out to be made up of tightly packed leaves that are digesting human remains. The meerkats stay alive by only visiting the trees at night, but some human spent too much time in the central tree and suffered a fate that might be Pi's in time.[43] Pi concludes that "once the person had died and stopped moving, the tree must have slowly wrapped itself around the body and digested it, the very bones leached of nutrients until they vanished. In time, even the teeth [Pi finds inside each "fruit"] would have disappeared" (Martel 282). Thus the fantastic island can be understood as another minimalist version of our planetary lifeworld, in which plants and microbes "eat" the bodies of animals and other organisms. All creatures eat each other, and thus Pi's Hindu vegetarianism had been an illusory effort to live outside the bloody economy of carnivorous existence.

The horrors of Richard Parker's predation early in the lifeboat voyage were only a dramatic extreme of the tearing and rending of other bodies that cannibalism also represents and that is only a slower, less visible process for the vegetation of the island. Pi is too horrified to come to such a conclusion, however, and flees with his tiger companion as soon as he understands how the island ecology works.

Martel's horrific shipwreck story is enclosed at the novel's beginning and end by mild, ordinary scenes of Pi's adult life in a Canadian city with a wife, children, and pets. It is as if Martel wants us to understand that beneath the comfortable facade of modern human life lies a desperate struggle whose stark essentials may become our future. Even in orderly contemporary cities, we continue to be tacitly entangled in the simultaneously cooperative and violent relationships with other animals that were so clearly seen on the lifeboat and the floating island of algae.

Besides asserting the closeness and simultaneous alterity of humans and other animals, Martel's narrative answers a question Derrida raised in his 1997 Cerisy lectures on animals. Turning Heidegger's formulation on its head, he wondered what the world would be like if it were poor in animals. He wondered whether our species could exist alone. Pi Patel knows that the world would be unbearable without the others and that in fact he could not have survived without the tiger. In distress after a ship has passed by without ever seeing their lifeboat, Pi cries out, "I love you, Richard Parker. If I didn't have you now, I don't know what I would do. I don't think I would make it. No, I wouldn't. I would die of hopelessness" (236).

Conclusion

Merleau-Ponty wrote in his working notes near the end of his life that his goal was to restore to us the world of "the wild Being," showing how it is absolutely different from our representations, which cannot exhaust it but which all "reach" it in limited ways. "Moreover the distinction between the two planes (natural and cultural) is abstract: everything is cultural in us (our Lebenswelt is 'subjective') (our perception is cultural-historical) and everything is natural in us (even the cultural rests on the polymorphism of the wild Being)" (*VI* 253). As we have seen in the preceding chapters, his efforts to think his way toward this restoration offer a new orientation for our attempts to understand other animals, our place among them, and indeed the whole enormous earthly biosystem in which we move and interact with them. If we understand our intertwining with all the others—and the synergies among us which parallel the synergies among all the cells and symbiotic bacteria within our bodies—we can escape the sense of lonely isolation that Ionesco described as the quality of modern life. Part of our culture already operates according to this understanding, for as Donald Griffin explains, biological continuity is the fundamental assumption underlying much medical research on brain structures and functions, on the efficacy of particular drugs, on muscular activity and metabolism, and on and on ("Expanding Horizons" 290).

This continuity includes cognitive, communicative, and cultural behaviors, as Merleau-Ponty implied in much of his late writing and as we have seen that Griffin and other ethologists have been working to demonstrate in the past several decades. Merleau-Ponty wanted to explain how a kind of mute meaning or Logos is everywhere in the primordial or wild Being that is our only environment and that of every organism on the planet. The function of human language and culture is to make this meaning visible and to extend it. He said of language, and I believe implied about cultural creations more broadly, that we need "to take it in its living state with all its references, those behind it, which connect it to the mute things it interpellates, and those it sends before itself and which make up the world of things said—with its movements, its subtleties, its reversals, its life, which expresses and multiplies tenfold the life of the bare things. Language is a life, is our life, and the life of the things" (VI 125).

For the most part, I would say, we seem to assume that we are talking primarily to ourselves, expressing aspects of the Logos immanent in the world, multiplying the life of the things so that we can more fully understand and experience them. Extending these ideas from language to culture more broadly, who else would be reading what we write or looking at our paintings and sculptures, watching our films, listening to our music, engaging in our dancing? But we should think again. We cannot be so sure that we are alone in these activities, as I tried to indicate in chapter 2 when discussing the aesthetic creations of other animals and in chapter 3 when considering communications between apes and humans. Chimpanzees have learned to use American Sign Language to converse in simple ways with humans, and bonobos have learned to read lexigrams, to point to them to communicate desires and ideas to humans and other bonobos. They can draw these symbols on the floor with chalk to tell a human companion what they want to do, and they can understand and respond to human speech at the level of a two-and-a-half-year-old child.[1] Apes can become sophisticated television viewers who identify with other apes on the screen (Savage-Rumbaugh, "Bringing Up Kanzi" 45).

As Donald Griffin suggested, such recent developments in the study of animal communications have opened the way "to asking animals direct questions about their mental experiences and intentions" ("Expanding Horizons" 31). Merleau-Ponty was reading and discussing earlier ethologists such as Jakob von Uexküll, Konrad Lorenz, and Nikolaas Tinbergen who were already considering animal subjectivity and communication. Griffin, Penny Patterson, Sue Savage-Rumbaugh, Frans de Waal, and Irene Pepperberg, along with many other researchers, have been advancing these possibilities steadily. Near the end of *The Ecological Thought*, Timothy Morton offers seven humanist suggestions for scientists to consider in their experiments. Among these are the questions of whether animals enjoy art, whether animals can self-reflect, whether Neanderthals had imagination, and whether bacteria can suffer (114). In fact, as we have seen in chapters 2 and 3, scientists have been thinking about these questions and many others related to them for a very long time. Griffin's masterful survey in *Animal Minds: Beyond Cognition to Consciousness* covers a wide range of such work, de Waal's *Ape and the Sushi Master: Cultural Reflections of a Primatologist* provides a similar retrospective for primatology, and a wealth of related work can be easily found if humanists will begin to familiarize themselves with contemporary studies of animals the way Merleau-Ponty did in his own work. Some, such as musician and animal theorist David Rothenberg, have performed bold interdisciplinary experiments to interact aesthetically with other animals. Rothenberg discusses playing wind instruments with many kinds of birds in *Why Birds Sing: A Journey through the Mystery of Bird Song* and doing the same thing by playing his clarinet into an underwater speaker and recording the responses of orcas, dolphins, and whales, in *Thousand Mile Song: Whale Music in a Sea of Sound*.[2] Others are investigating the aesthetic creations of animals such as chimpanzees who paint and dogs who create geometric arrangements of objects.[3] Skeptics claim that these are only circus tricks, but there is no doubt about the aesthetic qualities of many kinds of animal dwellings, of the flocking and swarming behaviors of many organisms from birds to fish, and of many of their courting behaviors. In a multitude of species, coordinated group behaviors are in fact dances and, like the famous waggle dances of bees, have clearly communicative functions. If human exceptionalism can be set aside and biological continuity seriously explored, we may learn in time that many other animals participate—according to their own styles—in bringing forth or displaying aspects of the Logos of primordial being that Merleau-Ponty described for human language and art, and thus also expressing and multiplying the life of the bare things. Jean-Christophe Bailly describes the songs of each species, executing their own variations, describing—indeed *reading*—the landscape in "an itinerary, a traversal, a remembering." Some gregarious creatures have circumscribed space-time fields, while others extend theirs over great distances. "But in all cases the skein formed with the world, whatever its value of envelopement, will constitute a territory, a world; and the world is nothing other than the interpenetration of all these territories among themselves, nothing but 'the envelopment of the *Umwelten* in each other,' to borrow another expression from Merleau-Ponty" (50).

Wild animals of many species interact with each other in remarkable ways, such as the well-known "herding" and "milking" of aphids practiced among some species of ants, for example, or parasitic small fish cleaning the body surfaces of larger animals such as sharks and whales. On our own bodies, tiny insects clean our eyelashes and eat dead skin, while inside our mouths bacteria neutralize plant toxins and in our intestines they ferment unused energy, break down our food, train our immune system, and produce certain vitamins. Such invisible internal kinds of symbiosis are paralleled by many kinds of external relationships that are easy to see.

People who work closely with animals through training and traditional cooperative activities understand the profound ways in which different species can "read" and understand each other, communicate with each other, and engage in sophisticated relational behaviors that often seem to be graceful forms of choreography. Donna Haraway reminds us that "Earth's beings are prehensile, opportunistic, ready to yoke unlikely partners into something new, something symbiogenic" (*When Species Meet* 220). Thus they have been involved in a "*dance of relating*" or "flow of entangled meaningful bodies" over the heterogeneous dimensions of evolutionary time (25–26).[4] English national sheep-herding champion Derek Scrimgeour speaks of his work with his dogs as "a conversation or a dance" in which intricately coordinated movements are achieved with gestural, verbal, and whistle communication.[5] From my own experience in herding sheep with my Australian kelpies, I would go further and say that all three species are involved in this complex activity of muted predation which is genuinely graceful when shepherd and dog work with skill and respect for the sheep. It is an ancient adaptation of wild canid predation, with dogs moving around the flock of sheep as wolves do. The sheep watch them carefully to evaluate their intentions. Sheep judge the degree of danger posed by each particular dog and seek to maintain a "flight zone" or bubble of safety between themselves and the dog.[6] If the dog moves suddenly or crosses the edge of the flight zone, the sheep move away. The speed or violence of their movement is determined by the degree of their fear of the dog. If, on the contrary, the dog moves gently and respects the flight zone, the sheep accept its presence nearby. Herding dogs understand the flock's behavior and carefully evaluate the actions of individual sheep so that they can prevent escapes and shape forward movement. Skillful dogs subtly gesture with their bodies at the edge of the flight zone to manipulate the flock's fear and thus cause it to move in the directions signaled by the shepherd. At the same time, any group of sheep will watch the approach of a dog to "read" its intentions. They easily distinguish between a dog who will treat them respectfully and one who will not, between a strong but self-restrained dog and a weak or anxious one, or one with violent motives. The shepherd or handler must simultaneously be "reading" the behavior of sheep and dog in order to participate in and direct the process, so that all three species must be constantly "reading" each other and agreeing to cooperate with the human who attempts to direct them. When these relationships and communications are working well, all the bodies flow along together, and a large flock's movement can resemble that of a school of fish flowing together in the sea.[7]

Haraway describes similar intricate processes of communication and cooperation in the sport of agility in which human partners move swiftly and gracefully with their dogs around a course full of obstacles such as teeter-totters, A-frames that the dog must climb up and over, a line of closely arranged poles that require the dog to weave in and out between them, a tunnel, and a series of jumps. Honesty, precise communication, and mutual respect must be maintained between human and dog, with the dog's expertise respected but at the same time the human rules of the game consistently enforced (*When Species Meet* 208–228).

Subtle and complex modes of communication, many impossible for humans to detect, make such negotiations possible. As Thomas Sebeok says, humans are aware of only a tiny subset of the many sensoria that Heini Hediger and other researchers have found at play at the intersecting *Umwelts* of various species, for example, "olfactory, ultraviolet, ultrasonic, magnetic, electrical, solar, stellar, and lunar stimuli" (*Swiss Pioneer* 44). What happens when species develop communication and resulting cooperation while living in close proximity is more than simple signaling. It is what Vinciane Despret describes as animals from different species *being with* each other so fully that they physically parallel each other's movements with their different bodies and in a sense become each other, thus cooperating in profoundly harmonious ways. Despret asserts that talented riders make imperceptible, unintentional movements which are the same ones the horse performs, so that "both are cause and effect of each other's movements" and "both embody each other's mind" (115). As we saw in chapter 2, Despret suggests that this is the kind of subtle, two-way communication between human and horse that created the Clever Hans phenomenon. Haraway relates Despret's discussion of gifted riders and their horses to the "naturalcultural practice" of agility partnerships between humans and dogs as coperformance of movement through a physical space in which they are "apart from each other in differently choreographed and emergent patternings" (*When Species Meet* 229). Despret sees similarly harmonized and overlapping ways of being in Konrad Lorenz's relationships with his geese and jackdaws, claiming that he constructs a "being with" that "sheds light on one of the ways bodies and worlds articulate each other" (130–131). This is an opening to and sharing with other creatures in a mode of emergent mutual experience like that Merleau-Ponty described as the synergy among different organisms whose landscapes interweave and whose actions and passions fit together exactly (*VI* 142).

As mentioned briefly in the preceding chapter, the new field of biosemiotics, which grew out of Uexküll's *Umwelt* theory, Peirce's linguistic philosophy, and Sebeok's establishment of zoosemiotics, is rapidly developing to provide extensive support for Merleau-Ponty's ontological assertions about the Logos immanent in the wild environment where we find ourselves. The silent language of primordial being which he described is being revealed by researchers all through the life sciences, as Jesper Hoffmeyer carefully explains in his recent book *Biosemiotics: An Examination into the Signs of Life and the Life of Signs*.

Hoffmeyer assembles a wide array of contemporary knowledge from many branches of biology and chemistry in order to demonstrate the significance of the biosemiotic project for a whole new understanding of the natural world. He wants to demonstrate how this effort ranges from the analysis of "the *languaging* of the human animal" to analysis of "*courtship trembling* in the water mite," the "*logic of self-organization and emergence*," and the "*biosemiotics of modern petrochemical agriculture*." He seeks to "make clear all the conceptual links and unique level properties that come into play as we move from one of these phenomena to the other." Increasingly important in this process is the theoretical difficulty of making clear the interrelationships between insights from areas traditionally understood as scientific, on the one hand, with insights traditionally associated with the humanities on the other. All are necessary for developing "a *general semiotics* inclusive enough to conceptualize the human being as being not only *in* but also deeply *of* nature" (*Biosemiotics* xvi–xvii).

The first chapter of Hoffmeyer's investigation, "Surfaces within Surfaces," enlists Merleau-Ponty's philosophy to explain the semiotics of the skin and its centrality to an understanding of the self. Because the skin has both an inner and an outer side, the self can exist only insofar "as that which is inside contains an intentionality toward or reference to that which is outside" (*Biosemiotics* 26). The key point here is corporeality, which gives us our self in relation to others, as Merleau-Ponty explains by stating in *Phenomenology of Perception* that "others can be evident because I am not transparent for myself, and because my subjectivity draws its body along behind itself" (*PP* 368). The skin's communication both with the outside world (as in responding to cold or heat and ejecting waste fluids and chemicals from the body to its surface) and with the body's interior (as in giving us the sense of heat or cold, communicating pressures from contacts with objects or other bodies) literally makes us aware of who we are and where we are in the world around us. Without the skin, we would not have a boundary that distinguishes us from the air and energies and substances in our environment. Indeed, our interior would just ooze into it, losing its human dimensions and cohesion. But at the same time, we would not have the awareness of what we move through and among. Indeed, Hoffmeyer sees the skin as a type of brain. "The skin keeps the world away in a physical sense but present in a psychological sense" (*Biosemiotics* 19).

As Hoffmeyer explains, our embodied being is far more complicated than we usually imagine. Under the skin are multiplicities of other cellular layers enveloping tissues and organs, so that beneath the most obvious surfaces are more and more surfaces descending into microscopic intricacies including single cells and then, within the cell, yet another group of biologically important surfaces. "The cell's interior is packed with bodies inside bodies, e.g. the organelles with names such as mitochondria, lysosomes, Golgi apparati, cell nuclei, and the endoplasmic reticulum.... Each human body consists of around thirty square kilometers of membranes, all exchanging molecular messages that bring the biochemical functions on the inside of these varying bodies into concordance with each other at a bewildering number of scales" (*Biosemiotics* 26–27).

This discussion begins Hoffmeyer's elucidation of a theory of semiotic emergence which implicitly extends Merleau-Ponty's chiasmic ontology of beings participating in the continued unfolding of Being in the Flesh of the world. Hoffmeyer presents this theory as a contrast to the Western tradition of positing "*virtual agents* whose forces are efficiently causal and yet unseen," from Adam Smith's invisible hand to Freud's Oedipal repression, behaviorists' conditioning and sociobiologists' selfish genes. Instead of such concepts that deny autonomy to the individual, "the idea of *semiotic emergence* implies that while there is no centralized director 'behind' the person or organism, the organism or person as an entity is continuously regenerated as an active, creative authority. *The person is thus not a stable being but rather a constant becoming.* The critical point is to recognize the emergent autonomy of various levels of organization" (*Biosemiotics* 28).

The book moves to consider how genes work within the body, how organisms evolved from single-celled to complex multicellular creatures, the semiotics of heredity and ontogeny, the development of the individual brain, zoosemiotics, metabolic codes, "ecological endosemiotics," the human place among other animals, the emergence of language, and finally perspectives on experimental biology, aesthetics, ethics, medical bioethics, cognitive science, and biosemiotic technologies. This ambitious biosemiotic synthesis is only the beginning of possible efforts to continue Merleau-Ponty's unfinished project of redefining nature, with its immanent Logos and wildness, and "the man-animality intertwining" that is our condition. Humanists can work with Merleau-Ponty's philosophy and take seriously its modeling of thoughtful engagement with the life sciences, at the same time learning from Hoffmeyer's challenge that we "learn to *speak with nature* in its own language" (*Biosemiotics* 354), as his book tries to demonstrate we can.

Cary Wolfe has said that we need an ontology that takes the body as central.[8] I trust I have been able to show that Merleau-Ponty gave us such a philosophy more than fifty years ago. From *Phenomenology of Perception* in 1945 through his final work in the 1950s and 1960s in defining his chiasmic ontology of the man-animality intertwining and exploring the meaning of the life sciences, animal studies, and evolution in the *Nature* lectures, he shaped a whole new sense of who we are and where we are in the life of the planet. He said, "Thus the body *stands* before the world and the world upright before it, and between them there is a relation that is one of embrace" (*VI* 271).

Notes

Introduction

1. Eugene Ionesco, quoted in Ronald L. Wallace, *Those Who Have Vanished: An Introduction to Prehistory* (Homewood, IL: Dorsey, 1983), vii; Jacques Derrida, *The Animal That Therefore I Am*, trans. David Wills (New York: Fordham University Press, 2008), 3–4, 54. Further citations of the Derrida book appear parenthetically in the text.

2. Cary Wolfe, introduction to *Zoontologies: The Question of the Animal*, ed. Cary Wolfe (Minneapolis: University of Minnesota Press, 2003), xi. Further citations of this work appear parenthetically in the text.

3. Val Plumwood, "Nature, Self, and Gender: Feminism, Environmental Philosophy, and the Critique of Rationalism," in *Ecological Feminist Philosophies*, ed. Karen J. Warren (Bloomington: Indiana University Press, 1996), 172–173. Further citations of this work appear parenthetically in the text.

4. Jacques Derrida, *Of Grammatology* (Baltimore: Johns Hopkins University Press, 1976), 48.

5. Susan McHugh, *Animal Stories: Narrating across Species Lines* (Minneapolis: University of Minnesota Press, 2011), 2.

6. Maurice Merleau-Ponty, *Phenomenology of Perception*, trans. Donald A. Landes (New York: Routledge, 2012), lxxxiv; originally published in French in 1945. Further citations of this work appear parenthetically in the text as *PP*.

7. Maurice Merleau-Ponty, *Nature: Course Notes from the Collège de France*, comp. and notes Dominique Séglard, trans. Robert Vallier

(Evanston, IL: Northwestern University Press, 2003), 166. Further citations of this work appear parenthetically in the text as *N*.

8. Maurice Merleau-Ponty, "Working Notes," in *The Visible and the Invisible*, ed. Claude Lefort, trans. Alphonso Lingus (Evanston, IL: Northwestern University Press, 1973), 274. Further citations of *The Visible and the Invisible* appear parenthetically in the text as *VI*.

9. See Frans de Waal, *The Ape and the Sushi Master: Cultural Reflections of a Primatologist* (New York: Basic Books, 2001), 71–77; Jesper Hoffmeyer, *Biosemiotics: The Signs of Life and the Life of Signs* (Scranton, PA: University of Scranton Press, 2008), xv–xvi, 174–775; and Timothy Morton's flat assertion that accusing others of anthropocentrism is itself nothing but anthropocentrism, in *The Ecological Thought* (Cambridge, MA: Harvard University Press, 2010), 75–76. Further citations of these works appear parenthetically in the text.

10. Jakob von Uexküll, *A Stroll through the Worlds of Animals and Men*, in *Instinctive Behavior: The Development of a Modern Concept*, ed. and trans. Claire H. Schiller (New York: International Universities Press, 1957), 5–29. Further citations of this work appear parenthetically in the text. This translation preserves Uexküll's use of the word *Umwelt*, which has become an important specific concept in animal studies, whereas the 2010 translation by Joseph D. O'Neil (*A Foray into the Worlds of Animals and Humans, with A Theory of Meaning* [Minneapolis: University of Minnesota Press]) uses the more generalized English term "environment" and thus loses Uexküll's precise meaning; compare 42–70 of this translation.

11. In 2002, the Merleau-Ponty Circle focused its annual conference on the philosopher's relation to ecology. The resulting collection of selected papers was edited by Suzanne Cataldi and William Hamrick and published in 2007 as *Merleau-Ponty and Environmental Philosophy: Dwelling on the Landscapes of Thought* (Albany: State University of New York Press, 2007). The first monograph to evaluate Merleau-Ponty as an environmental philosopher is Ted Toadvine's *Merleau-Ponty's Philosophy of Nature* (Evanston, IL: Northwestern University Press, 2009). Further citations of the Toadvine book appear parenthetically in the text.

12. Tim Ingold, *The Perception of the Environment: Essays on Livelihood, Dwelling, and Skill* (New York: Routledge, 2000), 2–3. Further citations of this work appear parenthetically in the text. Ingold acknowledges the influence of Merleau-Ponty's work, for example, in notes to chapter 1, chapter 9, and chapter 23: 420, 423, 428, and 435.

13. See also Ursula Heise's "A Hitchhiker's Guide to Ecocriticism," *PMLA* 121 (March 2006): 509–510.

14. James Lovelock, *The Ages of Gaia: A Biography of Our Living Earth* (1988; repr., New York: Bantam, 1990), 236.

15. James Lovelock, *The Revenge of Gaia: Earth's Climate Crisis and the Fate of Humanity* (New York: Basic Books, 2006), 153. Further citations of this work appear parenthetically in the text.

16. Jean-Christophe Bailly, *The Animal Side*, trans. Catherine Porter (New York: Fordham University Press, 2011), 14–15, 49–50, 72–75. Further citations of this work appear parenthetically in the text.

1. A Philosophy of Life

1. Mark Johnson, *The Meaning of the Body: Aesthetics and Human Understanding* (Chicago: University of Chicago Press, 2007), 2. Further citations of this work appear parenthetically in the text.

2. Giovanni Pico della Mirandola, *Oration on the Dignity of Man* (1486), trans. A. Robert Caponigri (South Bend, IN: Regenry/Gateway, 1956), 7–11.

3. Carolyn Merchant, *The Death of Nature: Women, Ecology, and the Scientific Revolution* (San Francisco: Harper and Row, 1980), 164, 194. Further citations of this work appear parenthetically in the text.

4. René Descartes, *Discours del la méthode pour bien conduire sa raison et chercher la verité dans les sciences/Discourse on the Method: of Conducting One's Reason Well and of Seeking the Truth in the Sciences*, ed. and trans. George Heffernan (Notre Dame, IN: University of Notre Dame Press, 1994), 35. Further citations of this work appear parenthetically in the text.

5. Dermot Moran, *Introduction to Phenomenology* (London: Routledge), 5. Further citations of this work appear parenthetically in the text.

6. Renaud Barbaras, *The Being of the Phenomenon: Merleau-Ponty's Ontology*, trans. Ted Toadvine and Leonard Lawlor (Bloomington: Indiana University Press, 2004), 320.

7. See also David Abram, *The Spell of the Sensuous: Perception and Language in a More-than-Human World* (New York: Pantheon, 1996), 40–43.

8. Charles Taylor, "Embodied Energy and Background in Heidegger," in *The Cambridge Companion to Heidegger*, ed. Charles Guignon (New York: Cambridge University Press, 1993), 317.

9. Matthew Calarco, *Zoographies: The Question of the Animal from Heidegger to Derrida* (New York: Columbia University Press, 2008), 147. Further citations of this work appear parenthetically in the text.

10. Greg Garrard, *Ecocriticism* (London: Routledge, 2004), 62–63, 111–112, 146; Garrard, "Heidegger Nazism Ecocriticism," *Interdisciplinary Studies in Literature and Environment* 17 (Spring 2010): 254, 261–263. Further citations of these works appear parenthetically in the text.

11. Martin Heidegger, *Poetry, Language, Thought*, trans. Albert Hofstadter (New York: Harper, 1975), 161.

12. Axel Goodbody, *Nature, Technology, and Cultural Change in Twentieth-Century German Literature: The Challenge of Ecocriticism* (Basingstoke, UK: Palgrave Macmillan, 2007), 129.

13. Jonathan Bate, *The Song of the Earth* (Cambridge, MA: Harvard University Press, 2000), 262. Further citations of this work appear parenthetically in the text.

14. Michael Zimmerman, *Heidegger's Confrontation with Modernity* (Bloomington: Indiana University Press, 1990), xvi–xxi; Zimmerman, *Contesting Earth's Future: Radical Ecology and Postmodernity* (Berkeley: University of California Press, 1994), 121; Zimmerman, "Heidegger's Phenomenology and Contemporary Environmentalism," in *Eco-Phenomenology: Back to the Earth Itself*, ed. Charles S. Brown and Ted Toadvine (Albany: State University of New York Press, 2003), 86–96.

15. Martin Heidegger, "Letter on Humanism," trans. Frank A. Capuzzi, in *Basic Writings*, ed. David F. Krell (San Francisco: Harper and Row, 1977), 205.

16. Martin Heidegger, "Building, Dwelling, Thinking," trans. Albert Hofstadter, in *Basic Writings*, 325. Further citations of this work appear parenthetically in the text.

17. Vandana Shiva, *Staying Alive: Women, Ecology, and Development* (London: Zed Books, 1988).

18. Donna Haraway, "Situated Knowledges: The Science Question in Feminism and the Privilege of Partial Perspective," in *Simians, Cyborgs, and Women: The Reinvention of Nature* (New York: Routledge, 1991), 188–189.

19. Monika Langer suggests that Heidegger's use of tropes for nature such as "home," "homelessness," "shepherd," "farmer," and "rootedness" subjectivize Being and make his thinking anthropocentric ("Nietzsche, Heidegger, and Merleau-Ponty: Some of Their Contributions and Limitations for 'Environmentalism,'" in Brown and Toadvine, *Eco-Phenomenology*, 114).

Michael Zimmerman fears that Heidegger's thought "may be consistent with modernity's project of the technological domination of nature" ("Heidegger's Phenomenology and Contemporary Environmentalism," 86).

20. Kate Rigby, "Earth, World, Text: On the (Im)possibility of Ecopoesis," *New Literary History* 34 (2004): 430.

21. David Ehrenfeld, *The Arrogance of Humanism* (New York: Oxford University Press, 1978).

22. Maurice Merleau-Ponty, "The Philosophy of Existence," in *Texts and Dialogues: On Philosophy, Politics, and Culture*, ed. and introd. Hugh J. Silverman and James Barry, Jr., trans. Michael B. Smith (Atlantic Highlands, NJ: Humanities, 1992), 132. Further citations of this work appear parenthetically in the text.

23. Lynn Margulis, *Symbiotic Planet: A New Look at Evolution* (New York: Basic Books, 1998), 3. Further citations of this work appear parenthetically in the text.

24. Steven Rose, *Lifelines: Biology, Freedom, Determination* (London: Penguin, 1997), 14–15. Further citations of this work appear parenthetically in the text.

25. Bruno Latour, *We Have Never Been Modern*, trans. Catherine Porter (Cambridge, MA: Harvard University Press, 1993), 16–27.

26. Richard Dawkins, *The Selfish Gene* (Oxford: Oxford University Press, 1989), 201.

27. Richard Lewontin, *The Triple Helix: Gene, Organism, and Environment* (Cambridge, MA: Harvard University Press, 2000), 129. Further citations of this work appear parenthetically in the text.

28. Ted Toadvine, "The Primacy of Desire and Its Ecological Consequences," in Brown and Toadvine, *Eco-Phenomenology*, 149. Further citations of this work appear parenthetically in the text.

29. For a fuller discussion of Merleau-Ponty's emphasis on embodiment, see Glen Mazis, *Humans, Animals, Machines: Blurring Boundaries* (Albany: State University of New York Press, 2008), 38–48. Further citations of this work appear parenthetically in the text.

30. Although Donna Haraway does not seem familiar with Merleau-Ponty's ontology, she expresses a similar sense of living interactions when she says that "the shape and temporality of life on earth are more like a liquid-crystal consortium folding on itself again and again than a well-branched tree," as in common notions of relationships (*When Species Meet* [Minneapolis: University of Minnesota Press, 2008], 31–32; further citations

of this work appear parenthetically in the text). Timothy Morton, also apparently unaware of Merleau-Ponty's concept of the Flesh, develops a concept of ecological interconnectedness which he calls "the mesh" (*Ecological Thought*, 28ff).

31. Alphonso Lingis, "Animal Body, Inhuman Face," in Wolfe, *Zoontologies*, 166. Further citations of this work appear parenthetically in the text.

32. David Abram, "Merleau-Ponty and the Voice of the Earth," *Environmental Ethics* 10 (1988): 101–120.

33. Louise Westling, "Virginia Woolf and the Flesh of the World," *New Literary History* 30 (1999): 855–875. Further citations of this work appear parenthetically in the text.

34. Eudora Welty, "The Wanderers," in *The Collected Stories of Eudora Welty* (New York: Harcourt, Brace, 1980), 439–440.

35. W. H. Auden, "A New Year Greeting," in *W. H. Auden: Collected Poems*, ed. Edward Mendelson (New York: Vintage, 1991), 837–839. Underneath the title, the following information appears in italics: "After an article by Mary J. Marples in *Scientific American*, January 1969." Auden clearly wanted to acknowledge his debt to the scientific article.

36. Thomas A. Sebeok, "Zoosemiotic Components of Human Communication," in *How Animals Communicate*, ed. Thomas A. Sebeok (Bloomington: Indiana University Press, 1977), 1062.

37. Jakob von Uexküll, "The Theory of Meaning," trans. Barry Stone and Herbert Weiner, in special issue, ed. Thure von Uexküll, *Semiotica* 42 (1982): 53.

2. Animal Kin

1. See, for example, Mary Midgley, *The Ethical Primate* (New York: Routledge, 1994), 128–133. Further citations of this work appear parenthetically in the text.

2. See Jacques Derrida, "Heidegger's Hand (*Geschlecht II*)," trans. John P. Leavey, Jr., in *Deconstruction and Philosophy: The Texts of Jacques Derrida*, ed. John Sallis (Chicago: University of Chicago Press, 1987), 161–196. Further citations of this work appear parenthetically in the text.

3. See Midgley's answer to the question of why philosophers are afraid to engage evolution in *The Ethical Primate*, 95–97. Also see Derrida's assertion in *The Animal That Therefore I Am* that neither Kant, Heidegger,

Levinas, nor Lacan "really integrates progress in ethological or primatological knowledge into his work" (95).

4. See Nicholas Wade, *Before the Dawn: Recovering the Lost History of Our Ancestors* (New York: Penguin, 2006), 14–33; Steven Mithen, *After the Ice: A Global Human History, 20,000–5,000 BC* (Cambridge, MA: Harvard University Press, 2004), 8–28; and Clive Gamble, *Timewalkers: The Prehistory of Global Colonization* (Cambridge, MA: Harvard University Press, 1994), 8.

5. Edward O. Wilson, "Biophilia and the Conservation Ethic," in *The Biophilia Hypothesis*, ed. Stephen R. Kellert and Edward O. Wilson (Washington, DC: Island, 1993), 32.

6. See Donna Haraway's lively discussion of this dynamic history, and her acknowledgment of Lynn Margulis and her son and collaborator Dorian Sagan's important related work, in *When Species Meet*, 30–33.

7. See Tim Ingold's chapter "From Trust to Domination: An Alternative History of Human-Animal Relations," in *The Perception of the Environment*, 61–76. Ingold argues that "the story we tell in the West about the human exploitation and eventual domestication of animals is part of a more encompassing story about how humans have risen above, and have sought to bring under control, a world of nature that includes our *own* animality" (61).

8. Richard Erdoes and Alfonso Ortiz, eds., *American Indian Myths and Legends* (New York: Pantheon, 1984), 97–105. Further citations of this work appear parenthetically in the text.

9. Frederick W. Turner III, ed., *The Portable North American Indian Reader* (New York: Penguin, 1974), 217–218.

10. Kenneth Hurlstone Jackson, ed., *A Celtic Miscellany* (Harmondsworth, UK: Penguin, 1971), 93–97. Further citations of this work appear parenthetically in the text. See also Paul Waldau and Kimberly Patton, eds., *A Community of Subjects: Animals in Religion, Science, and Ethics* (New York: Columbia University Press, 2006).

11. Maureen Gallery Kovacs, trans., *The Epic of Gilgamesh* (Stanford, CA: Stanford University Press, 1985), 29.

12. J. Donald Hughes, *Pan's Travail: Environmental Problems of the Ancient Greeks and Romans* (Baltimore: Johns Hopkins University Press, 1994), 32–33.

13. Stephen Mitchell, trans., *Gilgamesh: A New English Version* (New York: Free Press, 2004), 1–2.

14. It is important to understand the fragmented state of the text, which preserves the majority of the narrative in more than eighty clay tablets from

a number of different languages, with some key passages missing. Assyriologist and translator Andrew George is confident that as the number of tablets continues to increase with further archaeological discoveries, "our knowledge of the text will become better and better, so that one day the epic will again be complete, as it last was more than two thousand years ago" (introduction to *The Epic of Gilgamesh: The Babylonian Epic Poem and Other Texts in Akkadian and Sumerian* [London: Allen Lane, 1999], xiv). The historical King Gilgamesh lived around 2700 BCE, and the earliest written epics about him were produced about 2000 BCE, based on oral traditions (Kovacs, introduction to *The Epic of Gilgamesh*, xxi–xxiii). The languages and cultures encoded in the surviving texts are very different from our own, functioning according to symbolic economies and iconographies little understood in the modern era. Thus attempts at translation and interpretation will always be somewhat tentative. Primarily I quote from George's 1999 translation, a recent poetic effort to capture the meaning of the "Standard Version" compiled from the seventy-three extant Babylonian manuscripts. At some points, however, I also use N. K. Sandars's prose composite version, *The Epic of Gilgamesh* (1960; reprint, New York: Penguin, 1972), which pieces a fuller narrative together from the oldest Sumerian tablets as well as later ones including the Standard Version. Walter Burkert informs us in *Creation of the Sacred: Tracks of Biology in Early Religions* (Cambridge, MA: Harvard University Press, 1996), 60–61, that recently the older Sumerian version has been edited in full. But according to Andrew George, even the Sumerian version is still incomplete, as scholars in various parts of the world continue working to unite, edit, and translate the hundreds of fragments in many different countries (*Gilgamesh*, 141). Translations of the major Sumerian texts are published in George's edition (ibid., 145–208). In Sumerian versions, the goddess Ishtar bears her earlier name of Inanna, Gilgamesh is called Bilgames, and the monster guarding the cedar forest is Huwawa rather than Humbaba. Further citations of the epic appear parenthetically in the text.

15. See Stephanie Dalley, trans., *Myths from Mesopotamia: Creation, the Flood, Gilgamesh, and Others* (Oxford: Oxford University Press, 1989), 126n14, 127n24.

16. Donna Haraway, *Primate Visions: Gender, Race, and Nature in the World of Modern Science* (New York: Routledge, 1989), 133–185. Further citations of this work appear parenthetically in the text.

17. This is the interpretation implied in Maurine Kovacs's translation (*Gilgamesh*, 16–17) and in Stephanie Dalley's translation (*Gilgamesh*, 60). However, Andrew George translates the passage to describe Gilgamesh's performance of the *droit de seigneur* before the bridegroom is allowed access to his bride (*Gilgamesh*, 12, 15–16). See also Louise Westling, *The Green Breast of the New World: Landscape, Gender, and American Fiction* (Athens: University of Georgia Press, 1996), 20–21.

18. Sandars, *Gilgamesh*, 70–72; Burkert, *Gilgamesh*, 60; George, *Gilgamesh*, 20.

19. Jared Diamond, *Collapse: How Societies Choose to Fail or Succeed* (New York: Viking, 2005), 48.

20. Elizabeth Kolbert, "The Climate of Man—II: The Curse of Akkad," *New Yorker*, May 2, 2005, 64–66. Further citations of this work appear parenthetically in the text.

21. See Glen Love, *Practical Ecocriticism: Literature, Biology, and the Environment* (Charlottesville: University of Virginia Press, 2003), 83–88.

22. E. R. Dodds, ed., *Bacchae*, by Euripides (1944; reprint, Oxford, UK: Clarendon, 1960). Further citations of this edition appear parenthetically in the text as Dodds. Dodds explains in the introduction to his 1944 edition of the text that the formal qualities of this late play of Euripides are unusually archaic, marking it as the most ancient material the poet ever reshaped (ibid., xxxvi–xxxvii). The traditional nature of many scenes is attested on vase paintings that long predate Euripides (xxxiii–xxvi). It was one of the playwright's final works, written sometime between 408 BCE and his death in 406 (xxxix).

23. For a closely reasoned evaluation of Nietzsche's debt to Darwin, as well as his challenges to some Darwinian principles, see John Richardson, *Nietzsche's New Darwinism* (New York: Oxford University Press, 2004).

24. Friedrich Nietzsche, *The Birth of Tragedy* (1872), in *"The Birth of Tragedy" and "The Case of Wagner,"* trans. Walter Kaufmann (New York: Vintage Books, 1967), 37, 59, 46–47.

25. Robert Bagg, introduction to *The Bakkhai by Euripides*, trans. Robert Bagg (Amherst: University of Massachusetts Press, 1978), 14. Further citations of Bagg's edition of the play appear parenthetically in the text as Bagg.

26. N. G. L. Hammond and H. H. Scullard, eds., *Oxford Classical Dictionary*, 2nd ed. (Oxford: Oxford University Press, 1970), 187.

27. Arthur Lovejoy, *The Great Chain of Being: A Study of the History of an Idea* (Cambridge, MA: Harvard University Press, 1936), 24–66. Further citations of this work appear parenthetically in the text.

28. Michel de Montaigne, "The Apology for Raymond Sebond," in *The Complete Essays of Montaigne*, trans. Donald Frame (Stanford, CA: Stanford University Press, 1965), 330–331. Further citations of this work appear parenthetically in the text.

29. F. E. Halliday, *A Shakespeare Companion* (Baltimore: Penguin, 1964), 321; see, for example, William Shakespeare, *Hamlet*, in *The Riverside Shakespeare*, ed. G. Blakemore Evans et al. (Boston: Houghton Mifflin, 1974), IV.iv.32–39.

30. William Shakespeare, *King Lear*, in *The Riverside Shakespeare*, III.iv.107–108.

31. Charles Darwin, *The Descent of Man, and Selection in Relation to Sex* (Princeton, NJ: Princeton University Press, 1981), 2. Further citations of this work appear parenthetically in the text.

32. See Timothy Morton's discussion of Darwin's arguments on this score, in *Ecological Thought*, 71–72.

33. Mary Midgley, *Animals and Why They Matter* (Athens: University of Georgia Press, 1983), 13. Further citations of this work appear parenthetically in the text.

34. See also Giorgio Agamben, *The Open: Man and Animal* (Stanford, CA: Stanford University Press, 2004), 39. Further citations of this work appear parenthetically in the text.

35. William McNeill and Nicholas Walker, foreword to *Fundamental Concepts of Metaphysics: World, Finitude, Solitude*, by Martin Heidegger, trans. William McNeill and Nicholas Walker (Bloomington: Indiana University Press, 1995), xxi. Further citations of this Heidegger work appear parenthetically in the text.

36. Derrida sees Heidegger's philosophy as Cartesian and asserts that "Cartesianism belongs, beneath its mechanicist indifference, to the Judeo-Christian, Islamic tradition of a war against the animal, of a sacrificial war that is as old as Genesis" (*Animal*, 101). Matthew Calarco describes Heidegger as using Christian ideas about the place of the human (*Zoographies*, 20–21).

37. David Farrell Krell, preface to "Letter on Humanism," in Heidegger, *Basic Writings*, 191.

38. See Calarco's much fuller discussion of the philosophical intricacies involved in Heidegger's failed attempt to move beyond traditional humanism, in *Zoographies*, 43–53.

39. Martin Heidegger, *What Is Called Thinking?*, trans. J. Glenn Gray and Fred Wieck (New York: Harper and Row, 1968), 16.

40. Cary Wolfe, "Human, All Too Human: 'Animal Studies' and the Humanities," *PMLA* 124 (March 2009): 570. Further citations of this work appear parenthetically in the text.

41. See Marie-Louise Mallet's foreword to *The Animal That Therefore I Am*, ix.

42. Kelly Oliver, "Stopping the Anthropological Machine: Agamben with Heidegger and Merleau-Ponty," *PhaenEx* 2 (Fall–Winter 2007): 18–19.

43. Kelly Oliver, *Animal Lessons: How They Teach Us to Be Human* (New York: Columbia University Press, 2009), 208–210, 328n2.

44. Ursula Heise, "The Android and the Animal," *PMLA* 124 (March 2009): 503–510.

45. Susan McHugh, "Literary Animal Agents," *PMLA* 124 (March 2009): 487–495; Kimberly W. Benston, "Experimenting at the Threshold: Sacrifice, Anthropomorphism, and the Aims of Critical Animal Studies," *PMLA* 124 (March 2009): 548–555; Bruce Boehrer, "Animal Studies and the Deconstruction of Character," *PMLA* 124 (March 2009): 542–547; and Una Chaudhuri, "'Of All Nonsensical Things': Performance and Animal Life," *PMLA* 124 (March 2009): 520–525. McHugh's 2011 book *Animal Stories* takes these arguments much further in mapping overlapping and permeable species boundaries and agencies in modern and postmodern literature and popular culture that reflect shifts in cultural perspectives toward animals.

46. Timothy Morton, "Ecologocentrism: Unworking Animals," *SubStance* 37:3 (2008): 73–96. Morton's *The Ecological Thought* assumes a myriad of complex interconnections of all animal life within what he calls the "mesh" of life on the planet.

47. Taylor Carman and Mark B. N. Hansen, introduction to *The Cambridge Companion to Merleau-Ponty*, ed. Taylor Carman and Mark B. N. Hansen (New York: Cambridge University Press, 2005), 22.

48. Renaud Barbaras, "A Phenomenology of Life," in Carman and Hansen, *Cambridge Companion to Merleau-Ponty*, 208, 212 (emphasis added).

49. See Neil Browne, *The World in Which We Occur: John Dewey, Pragmatist Ecology, and American Ecological Writing in the Twentieth Century* (Tuscaloosa: University of Alabama Press, 2007).

50. Claude Lefort, "Editor's Foreword," in Merleau-Ponty, *The Visible and the Invisible*, xx.

51. Robert Vallier, "Translator's Introduction," in Merleau-Ponty, *Nature*, xiv. Further citations of this work appear parenthetically in the text.

52. Mark B. N. Hansen, "The Embryology of the (In)visible," in Carman and Hansen, *Cambridge Companion to Merleau-Ponty*, 251. Further citations of this work appear parenthetically in the text.

53. In *Animal Lessons*, Kelly Oliver offers an extended discussion of what she calls "the strange kinship" Merleau-Ponty defines between humans and other animals, in contrast to Heidegger's insistence on a radical discontinuity (208–228). She finds that Merleau-Ponty collapses the distinctions among species in order to focus on both kinship *and* divergence and to take the theories of Uexküll in a different direction so that human behaviors and environments are simply different themes or styles of behavior, among which consciousness is merely one element (211–225). Timothy Morton, without any apparent familiarity with Merleau-Ponty's work, goes further, insisting in *The Ecological Thought* that we think of other animals as "strange strangers," introducing this concept on p. 14 and continuing to develop it throughout the book.

54. Gilles Deleuze and Félix Guattari, *A Thousand Plateaus: Capitalism and Schizophrenia*, trans. Brian Masumi (Minneapolis: University of Minnesota Press, 1987), 21. I do not further engage Deleuze and Guattari's notions of "becoming animal" because I share Donna Haraway's deep reservations about their project. Their insistence on the white male subject as the very essence of subjectivity from which any person must move to "become" either some undifferentiated kind of animal or similarly debased category of femaleness or racial otherness seems to me outrageous. As Haraway puts it, this kind of position, as well as their contempt for domestic pets, offers a distinctively clear philosophical display "of misogyny, fear of aging, incuriosity about animals, and horror at the ordinariness of flesh" (*When Species Meet*, 30).

55. See Gabriel Dover, "Human Evolution: Our Turbulent Genes and Why We Are Not Chimps," in *The Human Inheritance: Genes, Language, and Evolution*, ed. Bryan Sykes (New York: Oxford University Press, 1999), 86, 90–91; and Hoffmeyer, *Biosemiotics*, 12–14, 96–103, 196–202.

56. My account of Merleau-Ponty's late work emphasizes the biological continuity of human relationships with other animals somewhat more than does Mark Hansen, who asserts in "The Embryology of the (In)visible" that human evolution is "an emergence from animality as a new form of *being a body*" (254). I would say that in Merleau-Ponty's account, humans never quit animality but remain fully intertwined with it. My position is close to that of Francisco Varela, whom Hansen cites as seeing other animals as having selfhood and intentionality in varying degrees (259). Indeed, this is the implication of Uexküll's description of the *Umwelt* in *A Stroll through the Worlds of Animals and Men*. Glen Mazis provides a very nuanced account of how Merleau-Ponty's philosophy implies animal sentience and its continuity with human animality (*Humans, Animals, Machines*, 169–207). Hansen argues that "only the human body both is itself *and* perceives itself to be the experience of being" ("Embryology of the (In)visible," 260), whereas I think Merleau-Ponty's work is open to the possibility of other animals also having such understanding, as Mazis suggests and as we shall explore in the next chapter.

57. Jakob von Uexküll, *Theoretical Biology*, trans. Doris L. Mackinnon (New York: Harcourt, Brace, 1926), 270–284; Uexküll, "Theory of Meaning," 30–31; Merleau-Ponty, *Nature*, 168.

58. My view is obviously different from Brett Buchanan's emphasis on the structural relation between organism and environment as the important element in Uexküll's influence on Merleau-Ponty's concepts of interanimality (*Onto-Ethologies: The Animal Environments of Uexküll, Heidegger, Merleau-Ponty, and Deleuze* [Albany: State University of New York Press, 2008], 146–149; further citations of this work appear parenthetically in the text). Glen Mazis calls attention to Merleau-Ponty's more open interpretation of Uexküll's *Umwelt* than Heidegger's, showing how it suggests many kinds of tacit understanding and creative agency that depend on each individual creature's subjective experience of its surround (*Humans, Animals, Machines*, 197–200).

59. Bryan Smyth, "Merleau-Ponty and the Generation of Animals," *PhaenEx* 2:2 (2007): 204.

60. Maurice Merleau-Ponty, *The World of Perception*, trans. Oliver Davis (New York: Routledge, 2004), 58.

61. Frans de Waal, *The Age of Empathy: Nature's Lessons for a Kinder Society* (New York: Harmony Books, 2009), 12. Further citations of this work appear parenthetically in the text.

62. Vicki Hearne, *Adam's Task: Calling Animals by Name* (1986; repr., Pleasantville, NY: Akadine, 2000), 58. Further citations of this work appear parenthetically in the text. Merleau-Ponty himself made a similar point in his 1948 radio talk on animals (*World of Perception*, 58).

63. Nicholas K. Humphrey, "Nature's Psychologists," in *Consciousness in the Physical World*, ed. B. D. Josephson and V. S. Ramachandran (New York: Pergamon, 1980), 60; quoted in Donald Griffin, *Animal Minds: Beyond Cognition to Consciousness* (Chicago: University of Chicago Press, 2001), 254. Further citations of the Griffin book appear parenthetically in the text.

64. See Susan Perry, "Are Nonhuman Primates Likely to Exhibit Cultural Capacities like Those of Humans?," in *The Question of Animal Culture*, ed. Kevin N. Laland and Bennett G. Galef (Cambridge, MA: Harvard University Press, 2009), 247–268.

65. Irene M. Pepperberg, *Alex & Me: How a Scientist and a Parrot Discovered a Hidden World of Animal Intelligence—and Formed a Deep Bond in the Process* (New York: Harper, 2008), 62–72. Further citations of this work appear parenthetically in the text.

66. See Frans de Waal and Kristin E. Bonnie, "In Tune with Others: The Social Side of Primate Culture," in Laland and Galef, *Question of Animal Culture*, 19–40.

67. Julio Mercader, Huw Barton, Jason Gillespie, Jack Harris, Stephen Kuhn, Robert Tyler, and Christoph Boesch, "4,300-Year-Old Chimpanzee Sites and the Origin of Percussive Stone Technology," *Proceedings of the National Academy of Sciences* 104 (February 2007): 3043–3048.

68. Russell P. Balda and Alan C. Kamil, "The Spacial Memory of Clark's Nutcrackers (*Nicifraga Columbiana*) in an Analogue of the Radial Arm Maze," *Animal Learning and Behavior* 16:2 (1988): 116–122.

69. Caitlin O'Connell, *The Elephant's Secret Sense: The Hidden Life of the Wild Herds of Africa* (New York: Free Press, 2007).

70. Francis Pryor, *Britain B.C.: Life in Britain and Ireland before the Romans* (New York: Harper, 2003), 119–121. Further citations of this work appear parenthetically in the text.

71. See photographs of some of the people I met, hunting with their dogs, at "Tribal Hunter Pictures: Hadzabe Tribe, Tanzania Photos," MaxWaugh.com, http://www.maxwaugh.com/tanzania07/hadzabe5.php.

72. Nicholas K. Humphrey, *A History of the Mind* (New York: Simon and Schuster, 1992), 192–193.

3. Language Is Everywhere

1. See Mark Johnson's deft summary of this situation in *The Meaning of the Body*, 1–3.

2. New research suggests that this is true even for earthworms: Matt Walker, "Earthworms Form Herds and Make 'Group Decisions,'" *BBC Earth News*, April 9, 2010, http://news.bbc.co.uk/earth/hi/earth_news/newsid_8604000/8604584.stm. (See April 2010 issue of the journal *Ethology*.)

3. Michael Tomasello, *Origins of Human Communication* (Cambridge, MA: MIT Press, 2008); Philip Lieberman, *Toward an Evolutionary Biology of Language* (Cambridge, MA: Harvard University Press, 2006); E. Sue Savage-Rumbaugh, Stuart Shanker, and Talbot J. Taylor, *Apes, Language, and the Human Mind* (New York: Oxford University Press, 1998); Terrence W. Deacon, *The Symbolic Species: The Co-evolution of Language and the Brain* (New York: Norton, 1997); Stanley I. Greenspan and Stuart G. Shanker, *The First Idea: How Symbols, Language, and Intelligence Evolved from Our Primate Ancestors to Modern Humans* (Cambridge, MA: Da Capo, 2004); Christine Kenneally, *The First Word: The Search for the Origins of Language* (New York: Viking, 2007). Further citations of these works appear parenthetically in the text.

4. George Lakoff and Mark Johnson, *Metaphors We Live By* (Chicago: University of Chicago Press, 1980); Lakoff and Johnson, *Philosophy in the Flesh: The Embodied Mind and Its Challenge to Western Thought* (New York: Basic Books, 1999).

5. Wendy Wheeler, *The Whole Creature: Complexity, Biosemiotics, and the Evolution of Culture* (London: Lawrence and Wishart, 2006), 19. Further citations of this work appear parenthetically in the text. See Tomasello, *Origins of Human Communication*, 13, for a biologist's similar view; and see also Hoffmeyer's description of genetic codes as semiotic and operating within organisms in a dynamic physical interplay that is essentially linguistic (*Signs of Meaning in the Universe*, trans. Barbara J. Haveland [Bloomington: Indiana University Press, 1996], 11–51; further citations of this work appear parenthetically in the text).

6. See also Edward O. Wilson, "Trailhead," *New Yorker*, January 25, 2010, 56–62.

7. E. Sue Savage-Rumbaugh, "Bringing Up Kanzi," in Savage-Rumbaugh, Shanker, and Taylor, *Apes, Language, and the Human Mind*, 63–64. Further citations of this work appear parenthetically in the text.

8. Penny Patterson's work with the gorilla Koko has elicited similar skepticism. See Dorothy L. Cheney and Robert M. Seyfarth, "Constraints and Preadaptations in the Earliest Stages of Language Evolution," *Linguistic Review* 22 (2005): 151–152; and Derek C. Penn, Keith J. Holyoak, and Daniel J. Povinelli, "Darwin's Mistake: Explaining the Discontinuity between Human and Nonhuman Minds," *Behavioral and Brain Sciences* 31 (2008): 121–122. Penn et al. are challenged by such assertions as José Luis Bermúdez's that their hypothesis only redescribes the phenomena it seeks to explain. See Bermúdez, "The Reinterpretation Hypothesis: Explanation or Redescription?," *Behavioral and Brain Sciences* 31 (2008): 131–132. Further citations of these works appear parenthetically in the text.

9. Jacques Derrida, "'Eating Well,' or the Calculation of the Subject: An Interview with Jacques Derrida," trans. Peter Connor and Avital Ronnell, in *Who Comes after the Subject?*, ed. Eduardo Cadava, Peter Connor, and Jean-Luc Nancy (New York: Routledge, 1991), 116–117.

10. Philip Armstrong, *What Animals Mean in the Fiction of Modernity* (New York: Routledge, 2008), 205. Further citations of this work appear parenthetically in the text.

11. Indeed, Povinelli goes so far as to deny that work such as Savage-Rumbaugh's with Kanzi or Patterson's with Koko counts as science. For him, they are only practicing circus tricks which cannot be experimentally replicated and create situations close to the relationship between the famous German horse Clever Hans and his handler ("Mental Evolution in Humans and Apes: Closing Remarks from New Iberia," lecture at the University of Oregon, Eugene, February 26, 2010). See also Cheney and Seyfarth, "Constraints and Preadaptations," 150–152.

12. Antonio Damasio, *Descartes' Error: Emotion, Reason, and the Human Brain* (New York: Penguin, 2005). 94. Further citations of this work appear parenthetically in the text.

13. E. Sue Savage-Rumbaugh and Duane M. Rumbaugh, "Perspectives on Consciousness, Language, and Other Emergent Processes in Apes and Humans," in *Towards a Science of Consciousness II: Second Tucson Discussions and Debates*, ed. Stuart R. Hameroff, Alfred W. Kazniak, and Alwyn Scott (Cambridge, MA: MIT Press, 1998), 546.

14. Victor Norris, "Bacteria as Tools for Studies of Consciousness," in Hameroff, Kazniak, and Scott, *Towards a Science of Consciousness II*, 402. Further citations of this work appear parenthetically in the text. See Damasio, *Descartes' Error*, 87, on the hormones, neurotransmitters, and

modulators in the bloodstream. In *Signs of Meaning in the Universe*, Hoffmeyer describes communication occurring everywhere in the "semiosphere" that suffuses the world, from electrical and chemical interactions to DNA-RNA dynamics and a myriad of communicative activities among organisms in the biosphere.

15. See Vinciane Despret, "The Body We Care For: Figures of Anthropozoo-genesis," *Body & Society* 10 (2004): 111–134 (further citations of this work appear parenthetically in the text); and Armstrong's discussion of David Premack's failure to consider the full cognitive possibilities of a chimpanzee's reaction to viewing, while confined in her bare laboratory cell, a film in which a wild orangutan was captured. Sarah, the chimpanzee, hooted and threw pieces of paper at the screen, aiming for the animal's captors, and then turned a terrified face to her trainer. Armstrong says, "Premack's protocols do not allow him to consider whether Sarah is alluding to her own memory of capture and, more strikingly, identifying empathetically with the experience of another animal, indeed a member of another species" (*What Animals Mean*, 208–209).

16. Cary Wolfe, "In the Shadow of Wittgenstein's Lion: Language, Ethics, and the Question of the Animal," in Wolfe, *Animal Rites* (Chicago: University of Chicago Press, 2003), 84.

17. Stuart Shanker, "Philosophical Preconceptions," in Savage-Rumbaugh, Shanker, and Taylor, *Apes, Language, and the Human Mind*, 138.

18. See Damasio, *Descartes' Error*; Lakoff and Johnson, *Philosophy in the Flesh*; Robin Dunbar, "Theory of Mind and the Evolution of Language," in *Approaches to the Evolution of Language*, ed. James R. Hurford, Michael Suddert-Kennedy, and Chris Knight (Cambridge: Cambridge University Press, 1998); Savage-Rumbaugh and Rumbaugh, "Perspectives on Consciousness"; Tomasello, *Origins of Human Communication*; de Waal, *The Ape and the Sushi Master*; and Kenneally, *First Word*. In *Art as Experience* (1934; repr., New York: Perigee Books, 1980), Dewey explains art as experience that is "prefigured in the very processes of living" (24).

19. Savage-Rumbaugh, "Bringing Up Kanzi," 12; Kenneally, *First Word*, 141–153. The issue is still a matter of debate, with such scientists as Dorothy L. Cheney and Robert L. Seyfarth claiming that apes have the physical ability but lack "a theory of mind" to recognize thoughts in others ("Constraints and Preadaptations," 151–152). Penn et al. concur ("Darwin's Mistake," 130–136), but Louise Barrett, José Luis Bermúdez, Derek Bickerton, and R. Allen Gardner critique their methods and conclusions

(Barrett, "Out of Their Heads: Turning Relational Reinterpretation Inside Out," 130–131; Bermúdez, "The Reinterpretation Hypothesis: Explanation or Redescription?," 131–132; Bickerton, "Darwin's Last Word: How Words Changed Cognition," 132; and Gardner, "Comparative Intelligence and Intelligent Comparisons," 135–136; all in "Open Peer Commentary," in Penn et al., "Darwin's Mistake").

20. See F. Eugene Yates, "On the Emergence of Chemical Languages," in *Biosemiotics: The Semiotic Web 1991*, ed. Thomas A. Sebeok and Jean Umiker-Sebeok (New York: Mouton de Gruyter, 1992), 471–486.

21. Hugh J. Silverman, "Translator's Preface," in *Consciousness and the Acquisition of Language*, by Maurice Merleau-Ponty, trans. Hugh J. Silverman (Evanston, IL: Northwestern University Press, 1973), xxxix. Further citations of this Merleau-Ponty work appear parenthetically in the text.

22. Jesper Hoffmeyer, "Some Semiotic Aspects of the Psycho-Physical Relation: The Endo-Exosemiotic Boundary," in Sebeok and Umiker-Sebeok, *Biosemiotics*, 102–103.

23. Kenneally discusses Terence Deacon's view that gesture was the evolutionary scaffolding on which language began to develop among our ancient primate ancestors (*First Word*, 246).

24. Greenspan and Shanker have recently posited the view that prelinguistic hominids engaged in a kind of bodily protoconversation of reciprocal emotional signaling, particularly between caregivers and infants, and that language has remained centrally emotional (*First Idea*, 194–195). Present-day work with young children who have severe language deficits relies heavily on "co-regulated affective gesturing" in order to help them learn to communicate (ibid., 195). See also Hoffmeyer, *Signs of Meaning in the Universe*, 110.

25. See Glen Mazis's emphasis on the emotional dimension of language acquisition and use in Merleau-Ponty's thought (*Humans, Animals, Machines*, 112–113).

26. See also Colwyn Trevarthen, "The Self Born of Intersubjectivity: The Psychology of an Infant Communicating," in *The Perceived Self: Ecological and Interpersonal Sources of Knowledge*, ed. Ulric Neisser (Cambridge: Cambridge University Press, 1993), 121–173; Mark Johnson on the absolute need of infants for warm interactive communication with caregivers if they are to survive (*Meaning of the Body*, 34–45); Greenspan and Shanker, *First Idea*, 194–195; and Tomasello, *Origins of Human Communication*, 59–99.

27. Kenneally comments on developmental psychologists' present theory of the cross-modality of language that causes it to emerge "in the child as an

expression of its entire body, articulating both limbs and mouth at the same time" (*First Word*, 134).

28. See also Irene Pepperberg's description of her indirect, social method of teaching Alex to speak (*Alex & Me*, 62–72).

29. Despret goes on to discuss the case of experiments with laboratory rats, demonstrating the radically different results from experiments depending on the expectations of the experimenter, which were transmitted unintentionally by the behavior of the humans to the rats. She discusses the effect of trust and affectionate relationship between humans and other animals, concluding that "to 'de-passion' knowledge does not give us a more objective world, it just gives us a world 'without us'; and therefore, without 'them'" ("The Body We Care For," 131). Such a world becomes impoverished, of bodies without minds or hearts, expectations or interests. This is exactly Vicki Hearne's point about behaviorist practices that prevent successful animal training (*Adam's Task*, 58; see previous chapter).

30. As we saw in chapter 2, Francis Pryor describes these developments as gradual, moving from dogs accompanying humans for random predation, as people followed and even lived alongside herds of prey such as reindeer during certain periods of seasonal migration, to "loose herding," involving control at certain periods in order to separate young animals after weaning into new herds for particular uses, and finally evolving into the "close herding" practiced in historical times and at present (*Britain B.C.*, 124–126; see also 71 and 84). Nerissa Russell surveys recent debates about this evolving process in "The Wild Side of Animal Domestication," *Society and Animals* 10:3 (2002): 285–302.

31. David Anthony, *The Horse, the Wheel, and Language: How Bronze-Age Riders from the Eurasian Steppes Shaped the Modern World* (Princeton, NJ: Princeton University Press, 2007), 221; David Anthony and Dorcas R. Brown, "Horses and Humans in Antiquity," *Eurasian Steppe Archaeological Research* website, http://users.hartwick.edu/anthonyd/harnessing%20horsepower.html.

32. Jesper Hoffmeyer, "Semiotics of Nature," in *The Routledge Companion to Semiotics*, ed. Paul Cobley (London: Routledge, 2010), 32–33.

33. Maurice Merleau-Ponty, *Signs*, trans. Richard C. McCleary (Evanston, IL: Northwestern University Press, 1964), 17.

34. Ted Toadvine's careful examination of Merleau-Ponty's views on animal access to language, in *Merleau-Ponty's Philosophy of Nature* (89–96), does not posit as full a linguistic or communicative synergy among animals

as I am suggesting. Indeed, he does not believe that Merleau-Ponty extended the kind of self-reflexive thought to other animals that he described for humans as the basis of our language.

35. Donald Griffin, "Expanding Horizons in Animal Communication Behavior," in *How Animals Communicate*, ed. Thomas A. Sebeok (Bloomington: Indiana University Press, 1977), 30–31. Further citations of this work appear parenthetically in the text.

36. Yann Martel, *Life of Pi* (Edinburgh, UK: Cannongate, 2002). Further citations of this work appear parenthetically in the text.

37. See Randy Malamud's *Reading Zoos: Representations of Animals and Captivity* (New York: NYU Press, 1998), which offers a devastating analysis of the long history of human cruelty in capturing, caging, and torturing wild animals and of the complex psychological and cultural responses to them.

38. See Mary Midgley on the conceptual perils of the philosophical tradition of the lifeboat argument (*Animals and Why They Matter*, 19–21).

39. "Moving beyond" is my translation of the key term *dépassement* from the original passage in *La nature: Notes cours du Collège de France*, ed. Dominique Séglard (1968; reprint, Paris: Éditions du Seuil, 1994), 335; cf. "overcoming," in the English edition (*Nature*, 268).

40. Graham Huggan, "Postcolonialism, Ecocriticism and the Animal in Recent Canadian Fiction," in *Culture, Creativity and Environment: New Environmentalist Criticism*, ed. Fiona Beckett and Terry Gifford (New York: Rodopi, 2007), 170.

41. Cary Wolfe, "In the Shadow of Wittgenstein's Lion: Language, Ethics, and the Question of the Animal," in Wolfe, *Zoontologies*, 45.

42. Graham Huggan and Helen Tiffin, *Postcolonial Ecocriticism: Literature, Animals, Environment* (New York: Routledge, 2010), 172–173. They also point out Martel's intertextual engagement with other tales of cannibalism such as Poe's *Narrative of Arthur Gordon Pym* (173).

43. I cannot find support for Huggan and Tiffin's claim that the secret of the "fruit" refers to "the everyday horrors of human eating on an industrial scale" (*Postcolonial Ecocriticism*, 174), because Martel offers no evidence to counter Pi's conclusion.

Conclusion

1. Savage-Rumbaugh, "Bringing Up Kanzi," 69; E. Sue Savage-Rumbaugh, "The Gentle Genius of Bonobos," TED lecture, May 17, 2007, YouTube,

http://www.ted.com/talks/susan_savage_rumbaugh_on_apes_that_write.html.

2. David Rothenberg, *Why Birds Sing: A Journey through the Mystery of Bird Song* (New York: Basic Books, 2005); Rothenberg, *Thousand Mile Song: Whale Music in a Sea of Sound* (New York: Basic Books, 2008).

3. See de Waal on animal aesthetic activity and interests (*The Ape and the Sushi Master*, 151–176); and Barbara Smuts, "Donnie: Making Circle," Barbara Smuts's webpage, Department of Psychology, University of Michigan, n.d., http://sitemaker.umich.edu/barbara.smuts/making_circle.

4. In Haraway's discussion of companion species relationships (*When Species Meet*, 30–33, 287), she also credits the work of Lynn Margulis and Margulis's son Dorion Sagan on symbiotic developments on the evolutionary scale, in their book *Acquiring Genomes: A Theory of the Origins of Species* (New York: Basic Books, 2002).

5. Derek Scrimgeour, conversation with the author, Scio, Oregon, October 2007.

6. Zoosemiotician Thomas A. Sebeok calls this distance "the Hediger bubble" and applies it to human behavior as well as that of other animals, in "Zoosemiotic Components of Human Communication," 1063. Swiss ethologist Heini Hediger's work in the 1930s and '40s on the psychology of flight in wild animals established that the very definition of taming and subsequent domestication is the reduction or even elimination of the crucial distance that various animals feel the need to preserve before fleeing from others (described by Sebeok in *The Swiss Pioneer in Nonverbal Communication Studies, Heini Hediger (1908–1992)* [New York: Legas, 2001], 18–19; further citations of this work appear parenthetically in the text).

7. On many American farms, guard dogs of specially developed breeds such as the Great Pyrenees and Anatolian shepherd serve a different function, identifying themselves with the sheep, living among them at all times, and protecting them from predators. Sheep readily decipher the body language and behavior of these dogs, accepting them as companions, even in the same field where they may be moved from place to place by a border collie or kelpie. If the guard dog knows the herding dog and trusts it, then the guard dog will allow the herding dog to work.

8. Cary Wolfe, "Animal Studies, Biopolitics, and the Post-Humanities" (presentation at the University of Oregon, Eugene, April 22, 2010).

Bibliography

Abram, David. "Merleau-Ponty and the Voice of the Earth." *Environmental Ethics* 10 (1988): 101–120.

———. *The Spell of the Sensuous: Perception and Language in a More-than-Human World*. New York: Pantheon, 1996.

Agamben, Giorgio. *The Open: Man and Animal*. Stanford, CA: Stanford University Press, 2004.

Anthony, David W. *The Horse, the Wheel, and Language: How Bronze-Age Riders from the Eurasian Steppes Shaped the Modern World*. Princeton, NJ: Princeton University Press, 2007.

Anthony, David W., and Dorcas R. Brown. "Horses and Humans in Antiquity." *Eurasian Steppe Archaeological Research* website. http://users.hartwick.edu/anthonyd/harnessing%20horsepower.html.

Armstrong, Philip. *What Animals Mean in the Fiction of Modernity*. New York: Routledge, 2008.

Auden, W. H. "A New Year Greeting." In *W. H. Auden: Collected Poems*, ed. Edward Mendelson, 837–839. New York: Vintage, 1991.

Bagg, Robert, trans. *The Bakkhai by Euripides*. Amherst: University of Massachusetts Press, 1978.

Bailly, Jean-Christophe. *The Animal Side*. Trans. Catherine Porter. New York: Fordham University Press, 2011.

Balda, Russell P., and Alan C. Kamil. "The Spacial Memory of Clark's Nutcrackers (*Nucifraga Columbiana*) in an Analogue of the Radial Arm Maze." *Animal Learning and Behavior* 16:2 (1988): 116–122.

Barbaras, Renaud. *The Being of the Phenomenon: Merleau-Ponty's Ontology.* Trans. Ted Toadvine and Leonard Lawlor. Bloomington: Indiana University Press, 2004.

———. "A Phenomenology of Life." in *The Cambridge Companion to Merleau-Ponty*, ed. Taylor Carman and Mark B. N. Hansen, 206–230. New York: Cambridge University Press, 2005.

Bate, Jonathan. *The Song of the Earth.* Cambridge, MA: Harvard University Press, 2000.

Benston, Kimberly W. "Experimenting at the Threshold: Sacrifice, Anthropomorphism, and the Aims of Critical Animal Studies." *PMLA* 124 (March 2009): 548–555.

Bermúdez, José Luis. "The Reinterpretation Hypothesis: Explanation or Redescription?" *Behavioral and Brain Sciences* 31 (2008): 131–132.

Boehrer, Bruce. "Animal Studies and the Deconstruction of Character." *PMLA* 124 (March 2009): 542–547.

Brown, Charles S., and Ted Toadvine, eds. *Eco-Phenomenology: Back to the Earth Itself.* Albany: State University of New York Press, 2003.

Browne, Neil. *The World in Which We Occur: John Dewey, Pragmatist Ecology, and American Ecological Writing in the Twentieth Century.* Tuscaloosa: University of Alabama Press, 2007.

Buchanan, Brett. *Onto-Ethologies: The Animal Environments of Uexküll, Heidegger, Merleau-Ponty, and Deleuze.* Albany: State University of New York Press, 2008.

Burkert, Walter. *The Creation of the Sacred: Tracks of Biology in Early Religions.* Cambridge, MA: Harvard University Press, 1996.

Calarco, Matthew. *Zoographies: The Question of the Animal from Heidegger to Derrida.* New York: Columbia University Press, 2008.

Carman, Taylor, and Mark B. N. Hansen, ed. and introd.. *The Cambridge Companion to Merleau-Ponty.* New York: Cambridge University Press, 2005.

Cataldi, Suzanne, and William Hamrick, eds. *Merleau-Ponty and Environmental Philosophy: Dwelling on the Landscapes of Thought.* Albany: State University of New York Press, 2007.

Chaudhuri, Una. "'Of All Nonsensical Things': Performance and Animal Life." *PMLA* 124 (March 2009): 520–525.

Cheney, Dorothy L., and Robert M. Seyfarth. "Constraints and Preadaptations in the Earliest Stages of Language Evolution." *Linguistic Review* 22 (2005): 135–159.

Dalley, Stephanie, trans. *Myths from Mesopotamia: Creation, the Flood, Gilgamesh, and Others*. Oxford: Oxford University Press, 1989.

Damasio, Antonio. *Descartes' Error: Emotion, Reason, and the Human Brain*. New York: Penguin, 2005.

Darwin, Charles. *The Descent of Man, and Selection in Relation to Sex*. Princeton, NJ: Princeton University Press, 1981.

Dawkins, Richard. *The Selfish Gene*. Oxford: Oxford University Press, 1989.

Deacon, Terrence W. *The Symbolic Species: The Co-evolution of Language and the Brain*. New York: Norton, 1997.

Deleuze, Gilles, and Félix Guattari. *A Thousand Plateaus: Capitalism and Schizophrenia*. Trans. Brian Masumi. Minneapolis: University of Minnesota Press, 1987.

Derrida, Jacques. *The Animal That Therefore I Am*. Trans. David Wills. Foreword by Marie-Louise Mallet. New York: Fordham University Press, 2008. Originally published as *L'animal que donc je suis* (Paris: Galileé, 2006).

———. *Aporias*. Trans. Thomas Dutoit. Stanford, CA: Stanford University Press, 1994.

———. "'Eating Well,' or the Calculation of the Subject: An Interview with Jacques Derrida." Trans. Peter Connor and Avital Ronnell. In *Who Comes after the Subject?*, ed. Eduardo Cadava, Peter Connor, and Jean-Luc Nancy, 96–119. New York: Routledge, 1991.

———. "The Ends of Man." *Philosophy and Phenomenological Research* 30:1 (1969): 31–57.

———. "'Geschlecht': Sexual Difference, Ontological Difference." Trans. Ruben Berezdivin. In *A Derrida Reader: Between the Blinds*, ed. Peggy Kamuf, 380–402. New York: Columbia University Press, 1991.

———. "Heidegger's Ear: Philopolemology (*Geschlecht IV*)." Trans. John P. Leavey, Jr. In *Reading Heidegger: Commemorations*, ed. John Sallis, 163–218. Bloomington: Indiana University Press, 1993.

———. "Heidegger's Hand (*Geschlecht II*)." Trans. John P. Leavey, Jr. In *Deconstruction and Philosophy: The Texts of Jacques Derrida*, ed. John Sallis, 161–196. Chicago: University of Chicago Press, 1987.

———. *Of Grammatology*. Baltimore: Johns Hopkins University Press, 1976.

———. *Of Spirit: Heidegger and the Question*. Trans. Geoffrey Bennington and Rachel Bowlby. Chicago: University of Chicago Press, 1989.

Descartes, René. *Discours de la méthode pour bien conduire sa raison et chercher la verité dans les sciences/Discourse on the Method of*

Conducting One's Reason Well and of Seeking the Truth in the Sciences. Ed. and trans. George Heffernan. Notre Dame, IN: University of Notre Dame Press, 1994.

Despret, Vinciane. "The Body We Care For: Figures of Anthropo-zoogenesis." *Body & Society* 10 (2004): 111–134.

de Waal, Frans. *The Age of Empathy: Nature's Lessons for a Kinder Society.* New York: Harmony Books, 2009.

———. *The Ape and the Sushi Master: Cultural Reflections of a Primatologist.* New York: Basic Books, 2001.

de Waal, Frans, and Kristin E. Bonnie. "In Tune with Others: The Social Side of Primate Culture." In *The Question of Animal Culture*, ed. Kevin N. Laland and Bennett G. Galef, 19–40. Cambridge, MA: Harvard University Press, 2009.

Dewey, John. *Art as Experience.* 1934. Reprint, New York: Perigee Books, 1980.

Diamond, Jared. *Collapse: How Societies Choose to Fail or Succeed.* New York: Viking, 2005.

Dodds, E. R., ed. *Bacchae*, by Euripides. 1944. Reprint, Oxford, UK: Clarendon, 1960.

Dover, Gabriel. "Human Evolution: Our Turbulent Genes and Why We Are Not Chimps." In *The Human Inheritance: Genes, Language, and Evolution*, ed. Bryan Sykes, 75–92. New York: Oxford University Press, 1999.

Dunbar, Robin. "Theory of Mind and the Evolution of Language." In *Approaches to the Evolution of Language*, ed. James R. Hurford, Michael Suddert-Kennedy, and Chris Knight, 92–110. Cambridge: Cambridge University Press, 1998.

Ehrenfeld, David. *The Arrogance of Humanism.* New York: Oxford University Press, 1978.

Erdoes, Richard, and Alfonso Ortiz, eds. *American Indian Myths and Legends.* New York: Pantheon, 1984.

Gamble, Clive. *Timewalkers: The Prehistory of Global Colonization.* Cambridge, MA: Harvard University Press, 1994.

Garrard, Greg. *Ecocriticism.* London: Routledge, 2004.

———. "Heidegger Nazism Ecocriticism." *Interdisciplinary Studies in Literature and Environment* 17 (Spring 2010): 251–271.

George, Andrew, trans. and introd. *The Epic of Gilgamesh: The Babylonian Epic Poem and Other Texts in Akkadian and Sumerian.* London: Allen Lane, 1999.

Bibliography

Gillan, Garth. "In the Folds of the Flesh." In *The Horizons of the Flesh: Critical Perspectives on the Thought of Merleau-Ponty*, ed. Garth Gillan. Carbondale: Southern Illinois University Press, 1973.

Goodbody, Axel. *Nature, Technology, and Cultural Change in Twentieth-Century German Literature: The Challenge of Ecocriticism*. Basingstoke, UK: Palgrave Macmillan, 2007.

Greenspan, Stanley I., and Stuart G. Shanker. *The First Idea: How Symbols, Language, and Intelligence Evolved from Our Primate Ancestors to Modern Humans*. Cambridge, MA: Da Capo, 2004.

Griffin, Donald. *Animal Minds: Beyond Cognition to Consciousness*. Chicago: University of Chicago Press, 2001.

———. "Expanding Horizons in Animal Communication Behavior." In *How Animals Communicate*, ed. Thomas A. Sebeok, 26–32. Bloomington: Indiana University Press, 1977.

Guignon, Charles B., ed. *The Cambridge Companion to Heidegger*. New York: Cambridge University Press, 1993.

Halliday, F. E. *A Shakespeare Companion*. Baltimore: Penguin, 1964.

Hammond, N. G. L., and H. H. Scullard, eds. *Oxford Classical Dictionary*. Oxford: Oxford University Press, 1970.

Hansen, Mark B. N. "The Embryology of the (In)visible." In *The Cambridge Companion to Merleau-Ponty*, ed. Taylor Carman and Mark B. N. Hansen, 231–264. New York: Cambridge University Press.

Haraway, Donna. *Primate Visions: Gender, Race, and Nature in the World of Modern Science*. New York: Routledge, 1989.

———. "Situated Knowledges: The Science Question in Feminism and the Privilege of Partial Perspective." In *Simians, Cyborgs, and Women: The Reinvention of Nature*, 183–201. New York: Routledge, 1991.

———. *When Species Meet*. Minneapolis: University of Minnesota Press, 2008.

Hearne, Vicki. *Adam's Task: Calling Animals by Name*. 1986. Reprint, Pleasantville, NY: Akadine, 2000.

Heidegger, Martin. *Basic Writings*. Ed. David F. Krell. Trans. Joan Stambaugh, David F. Krell, John Sallis, Albert Hofstadter, and Frank A. Capuzzi. San Francisco: Harper, 1977.

———. "Building, Dwelling, Thinking." Trans. Albert Hofstadter. In *Basic Writings*, ed. David F. Krell, 319–339. San Francisco: Harper, 1977.

———. *The Fundamental Concepts of Metaphysics*. Trans. William McNeill and Nicholas Walker. Bloomington: Indiana University Press, 1995.

———. "Letter on Humanism." Trans. Frank A. Capuzzi. In *Basic Writings*, ed. David F. Krell, 193–242. San Francisco: Harper, 1977.

———. *Poetry, Language, Thought*. Trans. Albert Hofstadter. New York: Harper, 1975.

———. *What Is Called Thinking?* Trans. J. Glenn Gray and Fred Wieck. New York: Harper and Row, 1968. Originally published as *Was heisst denken?* (1952).

Heise, Ursula. "The Android and the Animal." *PMLA* 124 (March 2009): 503–510.

———. "A Hitchhiker's Guide to Ecocriticism." *PMLA* 121 (March 2006): 503–516.

Hoffmeyer, Jesper. *Biosemiotics: An Examination into the Signs of Life and the Life of Signs*. Scranton, PA: University of Scranton Press, 2008. Originally published in Danish, 2005.

———. "Semiotics of Nature." In *The Routledge Companion to Semiotics*, ed. Paul Cobley, 29–42. London: Routledge, 2010.

———. *Signs of Meaning in the Universe*. Trans. Barbara J. Haveland. Bloomington: Indiana University Press, 1996. Originally published as *En snegl pa vejen: Betydningens naturhistorie* (1993).

———. "Some Semiotic Aspects of the Psycho-Physical Relation: The Endo-Exosemiotic Boundary." In *Biosemiotics: The Semiotic Web 1991*, ed. Thomas A. Sebeok and Jean Umiker-Sebeok, 101–123. New York: Mouton de Gruyter, 1992.

Huggan, Graham. "Postcolonialism, Ecocriticism and the Animal in Recent Canadian Fiction." In *Culture, Creativity and Environment: New Environmentalist Criticism*, ed. Fiona Beckett and Terry Gifford, 161–180. New York: Rodopi, 2007.

Huggan, Graham, and Helen Tiffin. *Postcolonial Ecocriticism: Literature, Animals, Environment*. New York: Routledge, 2010.

Hughes, J. Donald. *Pan's Travail: Environmental Problems of the Ancient Greeks and Romans*. Baltimore: Johns Hopkins University Press, 1994.

Humphrey, Nicholas K. *A History of the Mind*. New York: Simon and Schuster, 1992.

———. "Nature's Psychologists." In *Consciousness and the Physical World*, ed. B. D. Josephson and V. S. Ramachandran. New York: Pergamon, 1980.

Ingold, Tim. *The Perception of the Environment: Essays on Livelihood, Dwelling, and Skill*. New York: Routledge, 2000.

Jackson, Kenneth Hurlstone, ed. *A Celtic Miscellany*. Harmondsworth, UK: Penguin, 1971.
Johnson, Mark. *The Meaning of the Body: Aesthetics and Human Understanding*. Chicago: University of Chicago Press, 2007.
Kenneally, Christine. *The First Word: The Search for the Origins of Language*. New York: Viking, 2007.
Kohler, Wolfgang. *The Mentality of Apes*. Trans. Ella Winter. New York: Harcourt, 1927.
Kolbert, Elizabeth. "The Climate of Man—II: The Curse of Akkad." *New Yorker*, May 2, 2005, 64–73.
Kovacs, Maureen Gallery, trans. and introd. *The Epic of Gilgamesh*. Stanford, CA: Stanford University Press, 1989.
Kull, Kalevi. "Semiotic Ecology: Different Natures in the Semiosphere." *Sign Systems Studies* 26:334–371.
Lakoff, George, and Mark Johnson. *Metaphors We Live By*. Chicago: University of Chicago Press, 1980.
———. *Philosophy in the Flesh: The Embodied Mind and Its Challenge to Western Thought*. New York: Basic Books, 1999.
Laland, Kevin N., and Bennett G. Galef, eds. *The Question of Animal Culture*. Cambridge, MA: Harvard University Press, 2009.
Langer, Monika. "Nietzsche, Heidegger, and Merleau-Ponty: Some of Their Contributions and Limitations for 'Environmentalism.'" In *Eco-Phenomenology: Back to the Earth Itself*, ed. Charles S. Brown and Ted Toadvine, 103–120. Albany: State University of New York Press, 2003.
Latour, Bruno. *We Have Never Been Modern*. Trans. Catherine Porter. Cambridge, MA: Harvard University Press, 1993.
Lefort, Claude. "Editor's Foreword." In *The Visible and the Invisible*, by Maurice Merleau-Ponty, ed. Claude Lefort, trans. Alphonso Lingis, xi–xxxiii. Evanston, IL: Northwestern University Press, 1973.
Lewontin, Richard. *The Triple Helix: Gene, Organism, and Environment*. Cambridge, MA: Harvard University Press, 2000.
Lieberman, Philip. *Toward an Evolutionary Biology of Language*. Cambridge, MA: Harvard University Press, 2006.
Lingis, Alphonso. "Animal Body, Inhuman Face." In *Zoontologies: The Question of the Animal*, ed. Cary Wolfe, 165–182. Minneapolis: University of Minnesota Press, 2003.
Love, Glen. *Practical Ecocriticism: Literature, Biology, and the Environment*. Charlottesville: University of Virginia Press, 2003.

Lovejoy, Arthur. *The Great Chain of Being: A Study of the History of an Idea*. Cambridge, MA: Harvard University Press, 1936.

Lovelock, James. *The Ages of Gaia: A Biography of Our Living Earth*. 1988. Reprint, New York: Bantam, 1990.

———. *The Revenge of Gaia: Earth's Climate Crisis and the Fate of Humanity*. New York: Basic Books, 2006.

Margulis, Lynn. *Symbiotic Planet: A New Look at Evolution*. New York: Basic Books, 1998.

Margulis, Lynn, and Dorion Sagan. *Acquiring Genomes: A Theory of the Origins of Species*. New York: Basic Books, 2002.

Malamud, Randy. *Reading Zoos: Representations of Animals and Captivity*. New York: NYU Press, 1998.

Martel, Yann. *Life of Pi*. Edinburgh, UK: Cannongate, 2002.

Mazis, Glen. *Humans, Animals, Machines: Blurring Boundaries*. Albany: State University of New York Press, 2008.

McHugh, Susan. *Animal Stories: Narrating across Species Lines*. Minneapolis: University of Minnesota Press, 2011.

———. "Literary Animal Agents." *PMLA* 124 (March 2009): 487–495.

Mercader, Julio, Huw Barton, Jason Gillespie, Jack Harris, Stephen Kuhn, Robert Tyler, and Christoph Boesch. "4,300-Year-Old Chimpanzee Sites and the Origin of Percussive Stone Technology." *Proceedings of the National Academy of Sciences* 104 (February 2007): 3043–3048.

Merchant, Carolyn. *The Death of Nature: Women, Ecology, and the Scientific Revolution*. San Francisco: Harper and Row, 1980.

Merleau-Ponty, Maurice. *Consciousness and the Acquisition of Language*. Evanston, IL: Northwestern University Press, 1973.

———. "Indirect Language and the Voices of Silence." In *Signs*, trans. Richard C. McCleary, 39–83. Evanston, IL: Northwestern University Press, 1964.

———. *La nature: Notes cours du Collège de France*. Ed. Dominique Séglard. 1968. Reprint, Paris: Éditions du Seuil, 1994.

———. *The Merleau-Ponty Reader*. Ed. Ted Toadvine and Leonard Lawlor. Evanston, IL: Northwestern University Press, 2007.

———. *Nature: Course Notes from the Collège de France*. Comp. and notes by Dominique Séglard. Trans. Robert Vallier. Evanston, IL: Northwestern University Press, 2003.

———. *Phenomenology of Perception*. Trans. Donald A. Landes. New York: Routledge, 2012.

Bibliography

———. "The Philosophy of Existence." In *Texts and Dialogues: On Philosophy, Politics, and Culture*, ed. and introd. Hugh J. Silverman and James Barry, Jr., trans. Michael B. Smith. Atlantic Highlands, NJ: Humanities, 1992.

———. *Signs*. Trans. Richard C. McCleary. Evanston, IL: Northwestern University Press, 1964.

———. *The Structure of Behavior*. Trans. Alden L. Fisher. Pittsburgh: Duquesne University Press, 2002.

———. *The Visible and the Invisible*. Ed. Claude Lefort. Trans. Alphonso Lingis. Evanston, IL: Northwestern University Press, 1968.

———. *The World of Perception*. Trans. Oliver Davis. New York: Routledge, 2004.

Midgley, Mary. *Animals and Why They Matter*. Athens: University of Georgia Press, 1983.

———. *The Ethical Primate*. New York: Routledge, 1994.

Mitchell, Stephen, trans. and introd.. *Gilgamesh: A New English Version*. New York: Free Press, 2004.

Mithen, Steven. *After the Ice: A Global Human History, 20,000–5,000 BC*. Cambridge, MA: Harvard University Press, 2004.

Montaigne, Michel de. *The Complete Essays of Montaigne*. Trans. Donald Frame. Stanford, CA: Stanford University Press, 1965.

———. *Oeuvres complètes*. Paris: Gallimard, 1962.

Moran, Dermot. *Introduction to Phenomenology*. London: Routledge, 2000.

Morton, Timothy. *The Ecological Thought*. Cambridge, MA: Harvard University Press, 2010.

———. "Ecologocentrism: Unworking Animals." *SubStance* 37:3 (2008): 73–96.

Nietzsche, Friedrich. *The Birth of Tragedy* (1872). In *"The Birth of Tragedy" and "The Case of Wagner,"* trans. Walter Kaufmann. New York: Vintage Books, 1967.

Norris, Victor. "Bacteria as Tools for Studies of Consciousness." In *Toward a Science of Consciousness II: The Second Tucson Discussions and Debates*, ed. Stuart R. Hameroff, Alfred W. Kaszniak, and Alwyn C. Scott, 397–405. Cambridge, MA: MIT Press, 1998.

O'Connell, Caitlin. *The Elephant's Secret Sense: The Hidden Life of the Wild Herds of Africa*. New York: Free Press, 2007.

Oliver, Kelly. *Animal Lessons: How They Teach Us to Be Human*. New York: Columbia University Press, 2009.

———. "Stopping the Anthropological Machine: Agamben with Heidegger and Merleau-Ponty." *PhaenEx* 2 (Fall–Winter 2007): 1–23.

Penn, Derek C., Keith J. Holyoak, and Daniel J. Povinelli. "Darwin's Mistake: Explaining the Discontinuity between Human and Nonhuman Minds." *Behavioral and Brain Sciences* 31 (2008): 109–178.

Pepperberg, Irene M. *Alex & Me: How a Scientist and a Parrot Discovered a Hidden World of Animal Intelligence—and Formed a Deep Bond in the Process.* New York: Harper, 2008.

Perry, Susan. "Are Nonhuman Primates Likely to Exhibit Cultural Capacities like Those of Humans?" In *The Question of Animal Culture*, ed. Kevin N. Laland and Bennett G. Galef, 247–268. Cambridge, MA: Harvard University Press, 2009.

Phillips, Dana. *The Truth of Ecology: Nature, Culture, and Literature in America.* New York: Oxford University Press, 2003.

Pico della Mirandola, Giovanni. *Oration on the Dignity of Man.* 1486. Trans. A. Robert Caponigri. South Bend, IN: Regenry/Gateway, 1956.

Plumwood, Val. "Nature, Self and Gender: Feminism, Environmental Philosophy, and the Critique of Rationalism." In *Ecological Feminist Philosophies*, ed. Karen J. Warren, 155–180. Bloomington: Indiana University Press, 1996.

Povinelli, Daniel J. "Behind the Apes' Appearance: Escaping Anthropomorphism in the Study of Other Minds." *Daedalus: Journal of the American Academy of Arts and Sciences*, Winter 2004, 29–41.

———. "Mental Evolution in Humans and Apes: Closing Remarks from New Iberia." Lecture at the University of Oregon, Eugene, February 26, 2010. Personal notes by L. Westling.

Pryor, Francis. *Britain B.C.: Life in Britain and Ireland before the Romans.* New York: Harper, 2003.

Rendall, Drew, John R. Vokey, and Hugh Notman. "Quotidian Cognition and the Human-Nonhuman 'Divide': Just More or Less of a Good Thing?" *Behavioral and Brain Sciences* 31 (2008): 144–145.

Richardson, John. *Nietzsche's New Darwinism.* New York: Oxford University Press, 2004.

Rigby, Kate. "Earth, World, Text: On the (Im)possibility of Ecopoesis." *New Literary History* 34 (2004): 427–442.

Rose, Steven. *Lifelines: Biology, Freedom, Determinism.* London: Penguin, 1997.

Rothenberg, David. *Thousand Mile Song: Whale Music in a Sea of Sound.* New York: Basic Books, 2008.

———. *Why Birds Sing: A Journey through the Mystery of Bird Song.* New York: Basic Books, 2005.

Russell, Nerissa. "The Wild Side of Animal Domestication." *Society and Animals* 10:3 (2002): 285–302.

Sachs, Oliver. *The Man Who Mistook His Wife for a Hat and Other Clinical Tales.* New York: Summit Books, 1985.

Sandars, N. K., trans. and introd. *The Epic of Gilgamesh.* 1960. Reprint, New York: Penguin, 1972.

Savage-Rumbaugh, E. Sue. "The Gentle Genius of Bonobos." TED lecture, May 17, 2007. YouTube, http://www.ted.com/talks/susan_savage_rumbaugh_on_apes_that_write.html.

———. "Bringing Up Kanzi." In *Apes, Language, and the Human Mind*, by E. Sue Savage-Rumbaugh, Stuart G. Shanker, and Talbot J. Taylor, 3–74. New York: Oxford University Press, 1998.

Savage-Rumbaugh, E. Sue, and Duane M. Rumbaugh. "Perspectives on Consciousness, Language, and Other Emergent Processes in Apes and Humans." In *Towards a Science of Consciousness II: Second Tucson Discussions and Debates*, ed. Stuart R. Hameroff, Alfred W. Kaszniak, and Alwyn Scott, 533–549. Cambridge, MA: MIT University Press, 1998.

Savage-Rumbaugh, E. Sue, Stuart G. Shanker, and Talbot J. Taylor. *Apes, Language, and the Human Mind.* New York: Oxford University Press, 1998.

Sebeok, Thomas A. *The Swiss Pioneer in Nonverbal Communication Studies, Heini Hediger (1908–1992).* New York: Legas, 2001.

———. "Zoosemiotic Components of Human Communication." In *How Animals Communicate*, ed. Thomas A. Sebeok, 1055–1077. Bloomington: Indiana University Press, 1977.

Sebeok, Thomas A., and Jean Umiker-Sebeok, eds. *Biosemiotics: The Semiotic Web 1991.* New York: Mouton de Gruyter, 1992.

Shakespeare, William. *The Riverside Shakespeare.* Ed. G. Blakemore Evans et al. Boston: Houghton Mifflin, 1974.

Shanker, Stuart. "Philosophical Preconceptions." In *Apes, Language, and the Human Mind*, by E. Sue Savage-Rumbaugh, Stuart Shanker, and Talbot J. Taylor, 77–138. New York: Oxford University Press, 1998.

Shiva, Vandana. *Staying Alive: Women, Ecology, and Development*. London: Zed Books, 1988.

Silverman, Hugh. "Translator's Preface." In *Consciousness and the Acquisition of Language*, by Maurice Merleau-Ponty, xxxiii–xl. Evanston, IL: Northwestern University Press, 1973.

Smuts, Barbara. "Donnie: Making Circle." Barbara Smuts's webpage, Department of Psychology, University of Michigan, n.d. http://sitemaker.umich.edu/barbara.smuts/making_circle.

Smyth, Bryan. "Merleau-Ponty and the Generation of Animals." *PhaenEx* 2:2 (2007): 170–215.

Sykes, Bryan, ed. *The Human Inheritance: Genes, Language, and Evolution*. New York: Oxford University Press, 1999.

Taylor, Charles. "Embodied Agency and Background in Heidegger." In *The Cambridge Companion to Heidegger*, ed. Charles Guignon, 317–336. New York: Cambridge University Press, 1993.

Taylor, Talbot J. "Rhetorical Inclinations." In *Apes, Language, and the Human Mind*, by E. Sue Savage-Rumbaugh, Stuart Shanker, and Talbot J. Taylor, 139–180. New York: Oxford University Press, 1998.

Toadvine, Ted. *Merleau-Ponty's Philosophy of Nature*. Evanston, IL: Northwestern University Press, 2009.

———. "'Strange Kinship': Merleau-Ponty on the Human-Animal Relation." In *Phenomenology of Life from the Animal Soul to the Human Mind: Book I, In Search of Experience*, ed. Anna-Teresa Tyeniecka, 17–32. Dordrecht, Netherlands: Springer, 2007.

———. "The Primacy of Desire and Its Ecological Consequences." In *Eco-Phenomenology: Back to the Earth Itself*, ed. Charles S. Brown and Ted Toadvine, 139–153. Albany: State University of New York Press, 2003.

Tomasello, Michael. *Origins of Human Communication*. Cambridge, MA: MIT Press, 2008.

Trevarthen, Colwyn. "The Self Born of Intersubjectivity: The Psychology of an Infant Communicating." In *The Perceived Self: Ecological and Interpersonal Sources of Knowledge*, ed. Ulric Neisser, 121–173. Cambridge: Cambridge University Press, 1993.

Turner, Frederick W., III, ed. *The Portable North American Indian Reader*. New York: Penguin, 1974.

Uexküll, Jakob von. *A Foray into the Worlds of Animals and Humans, with A Theory of Meaning*. Trans. Joseph D. O'Neil. Minneapolis: University of Minnesota Press, 2010.

———. *A Stroll through the Worlds of Animals and Men*. In *Instinctive Behavior: The Development of a Modern Concept*, ed. and trans. Claire H. Schiller, 5–80. New York: International Universities Press, 1957.

———. *Theoretical Biology*. Trans. Doris L. Mackinnon. New York: Harcourt, Brace, 1926.

———. "The Theory of Meaning." Trans. Barry Stone and Herbert Weiner. Special issue, ed. Thure von Uexküll, *Semiotica* 42 (1982): 42–85.

Vallier, Robert. "Translator's Introduction." In *Nature: Course Notes from the Collège de France*, by Maurice Merleau-Ponty, comp. and notes Dominique Séglard, trans. Robert Vallier, xiii–xx. Evanston, IL: Northwestern University Press, 2003.

Wade, Nicholas. *Before the Dawn: Recovering the Lost History of Our Ancestors*. New York: Penguin, 2006.

Waldau, Paul, and Kimberly Patton, eds. *A Community of Subjects: Animals in Religion, Science, and Ethics*. New York: Columbia University Press, 2006.

Wallace, Ronald L. *Those Who Have Vanished: An Introduction to Prehistory*. Homewood, IL: Dorsey, 1983.

Welty, Eudora. "The Wanderers." In *The Collected Stories of Eudora Welty*, 427–461. New York: Harcourt, Brace, 1980.

Westling, Louise. "Darwin in Arcadia: The Human Animal Dance from Gilgamesh to Virginia Woolf." *Anglia* 124 (2006): 11–43.

———. *The Green Breast of the New World: Landscape, Gender, and American Fiction*. Athens: University of Georgia Press, 1996.

———. "Virginia Woolf and the Flesh of the World." *New Literary History* 30 (1999): 855–875.

Wheeler, Wendy. *The Whole Creature: Complexity, Biosemiotics, and the Evolution of Culture*. London: Lawrence and Wishart, 2006.

Wilson, Edward O. "Biophilia and the Conservation Ethic." In *The Biophilia Hypothesis*, ed. Stephen R. Kellert and Edward O. Wilson, 31–41. Washington, DC: Island, 1993.

———. *Consilience: The Unity of Knowledge*. New York: Knopf, 1998.

———. "Trailhead." *New Yorker*, January 25, 2010, 56–62.

Wolfe, Cary. *Animal Rites: American Culture, the Discourse of Species, and Posthumanist Theory*. Chicago: University of Chicago Press, 2003.

———. "Animal Studies, Biopolitics, and the Post-Humanities." Presentation at the University of Oregon, Eugene, April 22, 2010. Notes by L. Westling.

———. "Human, All Too Human: 'Animal Studies' and the Humanities." *PMLA* 124 (March 2009): 564–575.

———. "In the Shadow of Wittgenstein's Lion: Language, Ethics, and the Question of the Animal." In *Animal Rites: American Culture, the Discourse of Species, and Posthumanist Theory*, 44–94. Chicago: University of Chicago Press, 2003.

———. "In the Shadow of Wittgenstein's Lion: Language, Ethics, and the Question of the Animal." In *Zoontologies: The Question of the Animal*, ed. Cary Wolfe, 1–57. Minneapolis: University of Minnesota Press, 2003.

———, ed. and introd. *Zoontologies: The Question of the Animal*. Minneapolis: University of Minnesota Press, 2003.

Woolf, Virginia. *Between the Acts*. New York: Harcourt, 1941.

Yates, F. Eugene. "On the Emergence of Chemical Languages." In *Biosemiotics: The Semiotic Web 1991*, ed. Thomas A. Sebeok and Jean Umiker-Sebeok, 471–486. New York: Mouton de Gruyter, 1992.

Zimmerman, Michael. *Contesting Earth's Future: Radical Ecology and Postmodernity*. Berkeley: University of California Press, 1994.

———. *Heidegger's Confrontation with Modernity*. Bloomington: Indiana University Press, 1990.

———. "Heidegger's Phenomenology and Contemporary Environmentalism." In *Eco-Phenomenology: Back to the Earth Itself*, ed. Charles S. Brown and Ted Toadvine, 73–101. Albany: State University of New York Press, 2003.

Index

Abram, David, 38
Acoma Pueblo people, 49
Agamben, Giorgio, 72
Alex (grey parrot), 93–94, 97, 103, 110
Amatruda, Catherine, 79
American Sign Language, 106, 130, 136
animal cognition and communication, 4
animal consciousness, 85, 88, 101
animal culture, 9, 85–86, 101
animal language studies, 9, 103–109, 113
animal question, the, 2, 8, 49, 64
animal studies (scientific), 4, 28, 64, 88–99
animality, 3–4, 8, 66, 69, 77, 79, 84, 87
anthropocentrism, 43
anthropomorphism, 5, 88–89
apes, 67, 95, 136
archaeology, 10
Aristotle, 37
Armstrong, Philip, 105, 125–126
artifact construction by animals, 96
As You Like It, 62
Auden, W. H., 8, 39, 41–43, 45–46
axolotl lizard, 79–80

baboons, 91, 94
Bacon, Francis, 15
Bagg, Robert, 57–58
Bailly, Jean-Christophe, 12, 138
Bakkhai, The, 8, 39, 49, 56–60
Bakkhus. *See* Dionysos
Barbaras, Renaud, 17, 75
Bate, Jonathan, 20 , 23
beavers, 96
Beckett, Samuel, 128, 132
bees, 93, 104–105, 138
behaviorism, 88–89
being, 19, 24, 26, 35, 122, 143. *See also* brute or wild being
Benston, Kimberly, 74
Bergson, Henri, 25
biological continuity, 4, 69, 77, 79, 138
biology, 17, 77–85
biosemiotics, 9, 11, 102–103, 113, 141–143
Bischoff, Th. L. W., 62
Bitterman, Mark, 93
body language, 115–116
"The Body as Expression, and Speech," 113
Boehrer, Bruce, 74
bonobos, 9, 94–95, 103, 115–116, 136
bowerbirds, 95
brain, evolution of, 105

Index

Bronze Age, 49
Brute being, 119–120
brute or wild being, 18, 26–27, 35, 60, 73, 135–136

Calarco, Matthew, 71–73
Carman, Taylor, 74
Carson, Rachel, 47
Cartesian animal-machine, 70
Cartesian science, 15–16, 28, 30, 78, 90, 108
Celan, Paul, 20
Celtic traditions, 49, 61
Chaudhuri, Una, 74
chiasm, 26, 33–34, 40–41
chiasmic ontology, 102, 143
chiasmic relationships, 76
chiasmos, 26
chimpanzees, 9, 47, 63, 67, 72, 91, 94–95, 97, 103, 115, 130, 136–137; Washoe, 130
Christianity, 13, 61
Clarissa Dalloway, 19
Clever Hans, 116–117, 140
coevolution, 13, 18, 35, 46, 89, 127
Coghill, G. E., 78–79, 84
cogito, 15, 33–34
Collège de France, 6, 8, 26, 75
common emotions and cognitive abilities among animals, 97. *See also* Darwin, Charles
Consciousness and the Acquisition of Language, 9, 110, 113–115
constructivism, 17
contingency, 29
cosmology, 10
Couvillon, Margaret, 93
critical animal studies, 8, 72–74
cross-species communication, 116–117, 119–120
"Curse of Akkad, The," 49–50, 55–56

Damasio, Antonio, 106–107
Darwin, Charles, 13–14, 45, 61, 63, 77, 101–102, 111–112, 118; common embryological development among animals, 63; common emotions and cognitive abilities among animals, 97; common morphology among mammals, 63; mechanistic Darwinism, 77; Social Darwinism, 71; Ultra-Darwinism, 30
Dasein, 19, 21, 24–25, 66–68, 70, 86. *See also* Heidegger, Martin
Dawkins, Richard, 10, 30
de Waal, Frans, 10, 63–64, 88–91, 93–95, 127, 137
deep ecology, 43
dehiscence, 77
Deleuze, Gilles, 77, 92
Demasio, Antonio, 10
Derrida, Jacques, 1–4, 9, 47, 64, 68–73, 105–106, 127, 131, 134; "as such," 70–71; biological continuity, 69, 71–72; *Dasein*, 70
Descartes, René, 6, 13–16, 31, 45, 62, 64, 70, 101
Despret, Vinciane, 116–117, 140–141
Dewey, John, 75, 109
Diamond, Jared, 55
Dionysos, 57–60
Dobzhansky, Theodosius, 16
Dodds, E. R., 58
dogs, 98, 110, 137, 139–140
dolphins and whales, 97
domestication of plants and animals, 117
Dreisch, Hans, 65
dualism, 5, 7, 13, 18–19, 21, 30–32
dwelling, 19–20, 21–24. *See also* Heidegger, Martin

écart, 34, 41, 77. *See also* dehiscence
ecocriticism, 2, 14, 20–21, 38

Index

École Normale Supérieure, 26
ecological interrelationships, 34
ecological philosophy, 75
ecological psychology, 7
ecophenomenology, 39, 43
ecopoetics, 20
Eddington, Arthur, 10
Ehrenfeld, David, 24
Einstein, Albert, 34
elephants, communication of, 103
embodiment, 5, 13, 31, 39, 142
embryology, 6, 8, 77; embryonic development, 78–80; embryo's formal anticipation of its future, 77–80, 84–85
Emerson, Ralph Waldo, 2
empiricism, 17. *See also* realism
Enlightenment, 13–14, 61–62, 125
environmental crisis, 14
Environmental Humanism, 2
Epic of Gilgamesh, The, 5, 8, 39, 49–56
ethnicity, 6
ethology, 6, 9–10, 64–65, 84
Euripides, 8, 39
European Renaissance, 47
evolution, 6, 25, 69, 73, 75, 78, 86–87, 103; evolution of consciousness among animals, 82; evolution of human language, 103; evolution of language, 109–110; evolutionary emergence of humans, 36, 86
evolutionary biology, 6, 9–10, 16, 28, 44, 63–64, 77
evolutionary continuity, 9, 85, 72, 101, 103

flesh, 6, 35, 76–77, 143
Fossey, Dian, 53, 127
Foucault, Michel, 74
Freud, Sigmund, 68, 143

Garrard, Greg, 10, 20–21
Gassendi, Pierre, 15

Genesis, 65, 70
Gesell, Arnold, 77, 79–80, 84
Gestalt psychology, 5, 26, 28
gestural communication, 113–117
Gibson, James, 7
Goodall, Jane, 10, 53, 90, 93, 95, 127
Goodbody, Axel, 19–20
gorillas, 67, 91, 94
Gould, Stephen J., 10
Griffin, Donald, 92–93, 95–96, 104–105, 124, 135–137
Guattari, Félix, 77, 92

Haeckel, Ernst, 16
Haldane, J. B. S., 16
Hamlet, 62, 45
Hansen, Mark, 74, 77
Haraway, Donna, 22, 52–53, 68, 73, 90, 128–129, 138–140
Harrison, Martin, 20
Hawking, Stephen, 10
Hearne, Vicki, 88, 108, 126–128, 131
Hediger, Heini, 140, 165n6
Heidegger, Martin, 2, 9, 16–27, 45, 47, 70, 72–73, 76, 92, 94, 101, 134; animals poor in world, 65–66, 83; "as such," 66; *Dasein*, 19, 21, 24–25, 66–68; dwelling, 19–20; *Fundamental Concepts of Metaphysics, The*, 65–67; "Letter on Humanism," 67; *Umwelt* theory, 83; *What Is Called Thinking?*, 67
heirogamy, 53
Heise, Ursula, 74
herding, evolution of, 98. *See also* sheep herding
Hobbes, Thomas, 30
Hoffmeyer, Jesper, 7, 9, 112–113, 118–119, 141–143
Holocaust, 20
Holyoak, Keith, 106

Homo erectus, 47
Homo habilis, 24, 47
Homo sapiens, 37–38, 47, 60
horses, 116–117, 140–141
Huggan, Graham, 132
Hughes, J. Donald, 50
human animality, 25
human evolution, 38, 47, 86. See also evolution
human exceptionalism, 60, 64, 73, 86, 92, 138
human language, 9, 104–105; evolution of, 103
human physiology, 28
human speech as gestural, 113–115. See also gestural communication
human-animality intertwining, 39, 49
humanism, 13, 36, 68, 74
Humphrey, Nicholas, 89, 93, 98–99
Husserl, Edmund, 8, 14, 16–19, 25, 27, 74–75
Huxley, Thomas Henry, 62

idealism, 5, 16–17. See also intellectualism
Imanishi, Kinji, 89, 94–95
incarnation, 25. See also embodiment
indeterminacy, 41
Industrial Revolution, 60
Ineinander. See intertwining
infant language acquisition, 114–115
Ingold, Tim, 7
Innana/Ishtar, 50, 52–53
intellectualism, 17. See also idealism
intersubjectivity, 17
intertwining, 86
"The Intertwining—The Chiasm," 102
Ionesco, Eugene, 1–2, 135
Ishtar. See Innana/Ishtar
Italian Renaissance, 13–14

Japanese primatology, 89–90, 94–95
Jaspers, Karl, 25
Jeans, James, 10
Jeffers, Robinson, 47
Johnson, Mark, 13, 102, 110
Jolly, Allison, 93
Joyce, James, 19

Kant, Immanuel, 16, 25, 64, 70
Kanzi the bonobo, 9, 93, 105–106, 109–110, 115–116
Kenneally, Christine, 109–110
King Lear, 54, 62
Kohler, Wolfgang, 95
Koko the gorilla, 106. See also Patterson, Penny
Kolbert, Elizabeth, 55

Lacan, Jacques, 64, 70, 74
Lakoff, George, 102
language, 101–125, 131, 136; definition of, 105–113; embodied approach to, 102–105, 113–115; human, 101–102; philosophical and poetic, 122–123
lateral kinship of humans and animals, 38, 86
Latour, Bruno, 30
Leakey, Louis and Mary, 90–91
Lebenswelt. See life world
Lee, Charles, 93
Leopold, Aldo, 47
Leopold Bloom, 19
Levinas, Emmanuel, 2, 64, 70
Levins, Richard, 112
Lewontin, Richard, 30–31, 83, 112
Lieberman, Philip, 110–111
Life of Pi, 125–134
life world, 17, 75
Lingis, Alphonso, 36, 46, 76
linguistic theories, 102–103

Index

literature, 121, 123–134
Logos, 3, 7, 31, 69, 78, 86, 101, 124, 136, 138, 141, 143
Lorenz, Konrad, 9, 37–38, 78, 84–85, 87, 137, 141
Love, Glen, 10
Lovejoy, Arthur, 60–61
Lovelock, James, 10–11
Lucy, 24

Malamud, Randy, 125–126
man-animality intertwining, 3, 6, 36, 128, 143
Marcel, Gabriel, 25
Margulis, Lynn, 10, 35, 46–47, 63
Martel, Yann, 9, 125–134
Marxism, 26
Maturana, Humberto, 108
Mazis, Glen, 73, 75, 87, 119
McHugh, Susan, 3, 74
McNeill, William, 65
medieval bestiaries, 61
Merchant, Carolyn, 15–16
Mersenne, Marin, 15
Midgley, Mary, 64, 72, 89, 93
Midsummer Night's Dream, A, 61
modernist fiction, 19
Montaigne, Michel de, 1, 5, 45, 61–62, 68–69, 97
Moran, Dermot, 17, 19
morphology argument, 63, 67–68
Morris, William, 21
Morton, Timothy, 11, 74, 137
music, 123–124

National Socialism, 19–21
naturalism, 17, 36
Nature, 3–4, 6, 28–29, 37–38, 47, 64. See also *Nature* lectures
nature, 28–29, 37–38
Nature, La, 6
Nature lectures, 3–4, 9, 75, 77, 87, 112–113, 117, 119, 144
"Nature and Logos: The Human Body," 76, 86
Nazism. *See* National Socialism
Neanderthals, 137
Neo-Darwinism, 71, 112
Neolithic era, 117
neuroscience, 5, 10, 28
New Physics, 16
Newgrange, 24
Newton, Isaac, 15, 62; Newtonian mechanics, 28
Nietzsche, Friedrich, 57
Norris, Victor, 108

Oliver, Kelly, 72
omophagia, 59
oral traditions, 49
orangutans, 67, 94

Pacific Northwest Indians, 49
painting, 122–124
Paleolithic cave paintings, 5
Paleolithic era, 117
Panbanisha, 9, 109
Pasteur, Louis, 46
Patterson, Penny, 137
Peirce, Charles Sanders, 111, 141
Penn, Derek, 106
Pepperberg, Irene, 93–94, 103, 137
Phenomenology of Perception, 5, 7–8, 9, 14, 16–19, 26–27, 32–34, 101, 113–114, 122, 144
phenomenology, 27–28, 31, 74–75
Phillips, Dana, 10
physics, 10, 28
Pico della Mirandola, 14–15, 45, 61
Plato, 13, 31, 60

Plumwood, Val, 2, 43, 71
PMLA animal studies issue of 2009, 74
positivism, 16–17. *See also* naturalism
posthuman, 74
postmodernism, 17
Povinelli, Daniel, 106
pre-culture in animals, 79, 82
primatoloy, 4, 52–53, 63–65, 70
primordial silence, 124
Proust, Marcel, 19, 123–124
Pryor, Francis, 98

quantum physics, 6, 10, 28
question-knowing, 5

realism, 5, 17
reductionism, 30
relativity theory, 10, 28
Renaissance humanism, 61
res cogitans, 45
res extensa, 45
reversibility, 33–34, 118–119
Rigby, Kate, 23
Robinson Crusoe, 130
Rose, Steven, 30–31
Rothenberg, David, 137
Rumbaugh, Duane M., 108, 127
Ruskin, John, 21
Russell, E. S., 38

Sagan, Carl, 10
Sartre, Jean-Paul, 25, 74
Savage-Rumbaugh, Sue, 103, 105–106, 108, 115–116, 127, 137
science, 27–31, 75, 86, 123
Scientific American, 42
scientific experimentation on animals, 74
Scrimgeour, Derek, 139
Sebeok, Thomas, 42, 111, 140–141

sedimentation of experience, 9, 114, 117–119
semiosphere, 111
semiotic behavior, 9
semiotic emergence, 143
Shakespeare, William, 61
Shanker, Stuart, 108
sheep herding, 139–140
Shinoda, Patricia, 93
Shiva, Vandana, 22
Skinner, B. F., 88
Smith, Adam, 143
Smuts, Barbara, 127
Smyth, Bryan, 87
sociobiology, 71
sparagmos, 59
Spinoza, Baruch, 6, 36
Steinbeck, John, 47
Stonehenge, 24
"strange kinship," 72
strange kinship of humans and animals, 77
Structure of Behavior, The, 26
Swiss Family Robinson, The, 130
symbiosis, 35, 41–43, 73, 77, 135, 138
symbolic behavior among animals, 82
synergies, 135

Taylor, Charles, 18
Teilhard de Chardin, Pierre, 38, 47, 77, 86
Tiffin, Helen, 132
Tinbergen, Nikolaas, 9, 137
Toadvine, Ted, 31–32, 72, 87, 120
Todt, Dietmar, 94
Tomasello, Michael, 127
tool use, animal, 9, 95–96

Uexküll, Jakob von, 4, 6, 9, 16, 37–38, 43–44, 65, 71, 78, 80–85, 92, 101–102, 107, 111, 137

Umwelt theory, 4, 6, 9, 41, 65, 78, 80–83, 85, 87, 92, 104, 107, 138, 140–141

Valéry, Paul, 102
Vallier, Robert, 76
Varela, Francisco, 108
Visible and the Invisible, The, 5–6, 8, 9, 26, 33–37, 42, 75–76, 101–102, 113, 117, 119, 122; "Working Notes," 118, 124
vitalism, 26
Von Frisch, Karl, 93, 104
Vulpian, Edme, 62

Walker, Nicholas, 65
Watson, John, 88
Welty, Eudora, 8, 39–41

whale and dolphin communication, 103–104
Wheeler, Wendy, 102–103, 112
wild being. *See* brute or wild being
wildness of Being, 76. *See also* brute or wild being
Williams, Raymond, 112
Wilson, E. O., 30. 47
Wittgenstein, Ludwig, 126, 131
Wolfe, Cary, 1, 68, 73, 108, 131, 143
Woolf, Virginia, 10, 19, 39, 47, 125
"Working Notes," 36
writing, 121–123

Zimmerman, Michael, 20
zoos, 125–126, 129, 131
zoosemiotics, 9, 11, 42, 143

groundworks |
ECOLOGICAL ISSUES IN PHILOSOPHY AND THEOLOGY

Forrest Clingerman and Brian Treanor, *Series Editors*

Interpreting Nature: The Emerging Field of Environmental Hermeneutics
　Forrest Clingerman, Brian Treanor, Martin Drenthen,
　and David Utsler, eds.

The Noetics of Nature: Environmental Philosophy and the Holy Beauty of the Visible
　Bruce V. Foltz

Environmental Aesthetics: Crossing Divides and Breaking Ground
　Martin Drenthen and Jozef Keulartz, eds.

The Logos of the Living World: Merleau-Ponty, Animals, and Language
　Louise Westling